SPIRITUAL CONDITIONING

THE SURPRISING PARALLELS BETWEEN AIR-CONDITIONING AND SPIRITUALITY

JITENDRA KHANNA

GRATITUDE

Writing this book has been a journey of profound self-initiation and self-realization, evolving into a theme of spiritual conditioning. After much inner reflection and a satisfying resolution, I arrived at this concept with immense gratitude for those who supported me along the way.

First, my heartfelt thanks go to my family, who stood firmly behind this vision, encouraging me through every stage of this journey. Their unwavering belief in me brought life to this work.

I am equally grateful to my close colleagues, whose inspiration and encouragement were the seeds that led me to put pen to paper. Their presence and support kept me moving forward, making this project possible.

A special note of gratitude goes to my esteemed mentor, Shri Gyan Chand Moudgil ji, who introduced me to the world of air conditioning and encouraged me to explore the harmony between my profession and the spiritual elements of life. His guidance has been instrumental in shaping this work.

My deepest thanks to Sooraj, whose creative expertise helped bring my dreams to life. His dedication and skill transformed this vision into a tangible book, breathing life into every detail.

Lastly, I express my sincere gratitude to all the mentors, spiritual guides, and the Almighty, whose blessings made this endeavour possible. I am truly fortunate to have such a remarkable support system, enabling me to share these insights and bridge my professional journey with the spiritual devotion I call "spiritual conditioning."

CONTENTS

INTRODUCTION

Spiritual Conditioning: Exploring the Interplay of Human Spirituality

With the completion of the 23 chapters exploring the intricate parallels between Air-conditioner systems and human spirituality, the book **"Spiritual Conditioning"** emerges as a profound exploration of the interconnectedness of the physical and metaphysical realms. Through detailed comparisons, insightful reflections, and practical applications, readers embark on a transformative journey of self-discovery and inner exploration.

Each chapter offers a deep dive into various aspects of both Air-conditioner systems and human spirituality, drawing parallels that illuminate the universal truths underlying both domains. From the regulation of temperature to the management of energy flow, from the importance of maintenance to the resilience in the face of adversity, the book covers a wide range of topics, offering readers a comprehensive understanding of the intricate interplay between the physical and the spiritual.

Throughout the book, readers are invited to reflect on their own lives and experiences, to contemplate the deeper meaning behind everyday phenomena, and to embrace the wisdom that lies within. Whether they are Air-conditioner professionals seeking new insights into their field or spiritual seekers looking to deepen their understanding of themselves and the world around them, "Spiritual Conditioning" offers a wealth of knowledge and inspiration to guide them on their journey.

Ultimately, "Spiritual Conditioning" serves as a reminder of the interconnectedness of all things and the inherent wisdom that permeates every aspect of existence. By exploring the parallels between Air-conditioner systems and human spirituality, the book invites readers to awaken to the profound truth of their own inner Spiritual Conditioning, guiding them towards a life of balance, harmony, and fulfillment.

INTERCONNECT BETWEEN AIR-CONDITIONING & SPIRITUALITY

The Role of Air-conditioning Technology in Human Comfort and Well-being

Heating, Ventilation, and Air Conditioning (Air-conditioning) technology plays a crucial role in maintaining human comfort and well-being by regulating indoor environmental conditions. From ensuring thermal comfort to improving indoor air quality, Air-conditioning systems are essential for creating healthy and livable indoor spaces. In this comprehensive overview, we'll delve into the workings of Air-conditioning technology, its importance for human comfort, and the evolving landscape of Air-conditioning systems across the globe.

Air-conditioning Technology: How It Works

Air-conditioning systems work by controlling temperature, humidity, and air quality within indoor environments. These systems consist of several components, each playing a vital role in maintaining optimal conditions:

1. Heating: Heating systems utilize various sources such as furnaces, boilers, or heat pumps to generate warmth during colder months. The heated air is distributed throughout the building via ductwork or radiant systems, ensuring consistent indoor temperatures.

2. Ventilation: Ventilation systems exchange indoor and outdoor air to replenish oxygen levels, remove pollutants, and control humidity. Ventilation can be achieved through natural means (e.g., opening windows) or mechanical systems such as fans and air handlers.

3. Air Conditioning: Air conditioning systems cool indoor spaces by removing heat and humidity. This process involves compressing and expanding refrigerant gases to transfer heat from indoor air to the exterior, resulting in cooler temperatures inside.

4. Air Quality Control: Air-conditioning systems often incorporate air filtration and purification mechanisms to remove contaminants such as dust, allergens, and airborne pathogens. Advanced filtration technologies, including HEPA filters and

UV-C light, help improve indoor air quality and protect occupants' health.

Importance of Air-conditioning for Human Comfort

Air-conditioning technology plays a pivotal role in enhancing human comfort and well-being in various ways:

1. Thermal Comfort: Air-conditioning systems maintain indoor temperatures within a comfortable range, ensuring occupants'

comfort and productivity regardless of external weather conditions.

2. Improved Air Quality: Proper ventilation and air filtration remove pollutants and allergens from indoor air, reducing the risk of respiratory problems and allergies among building occupants.

3. Humidity Control: Air-conditioning systems regulate indoor humidity levels to prevent mold growth, minimize moisture-related issues, and maintain a healthy indoor environment.

4. Energy Efficiency: Modern Air-conditioning systems are designed for energy efficiency, reducing energy consumption and operational costs while minimizing environmental impact.

5. Occupant Health and Safety: By providing clean, comfortable indoor environments, Air-conditioning technology promotes occupant health, safety, and overall well-being, particularly in commercial buildings, hospitals, schools, and residential settings.

Future Requirements and Innovations in Air-conditioning

As environmental concerns and technological advancements continue to shape the Air-conditioning industry, several trends and innovations are shaping the future of Air-conditioning systems worldwide:

1. Energy Efficiency: With a growing emphasis on sustainability and energy conservation, future Air-conditioning systems will prioritize energy efficiency through advanced controls, variable-speed technologies, and renewable energy integration.

2. Smart Air-conditioning Systems: The rise of smart building technologies and IoT (Internet of Things) connectivity enables the development of intelligent Air-conditioning systems capable of predictive maintenance, remote monitoring, and automated optimization for enhanced performance and energy savings.

3. Green Building Standards: Increasing adoption of green building standards such as LEED (Leadership in Energy and Environmental Design) and WELL Building Standard drives demand for Air-conditioning systems that prioritize indoor air quality, occupant comfort, and environmental sustainability.

4. Integration of Renewable Energy: Air-conditioning systems will increasingly incorporate renewable energy sources such as solar, geothermal, and wind power to reduce reliance on fossil fuels and mitigate greenhouse gas emissions.

5. Air Quality Enhancement: Advancements in air filtration, purification, and ventilation technologies will continue to improve indoor air quality, addressing concerns related to airborne pollutants, allergens, and infectious diseases.

Present Systems and Future Developments

Currently, Air-conditioning systems encompass a range of configurations and technologies tailored to diverse applications and environmental conditions:

1. Split Systems: Split Air-conditioning systems, comprising indoor and outdoor units, are commonly used in residential and small commercial buildings for heating and cooling purposes.

2. Packaged Systems: Packaged Air-conditioning systems, installed entirely outdoors, are suitable for larger commercial and industrial spaces, offering centralized heating, cooling, and ventilation capabilities.

3. Variable Refrigerant Flow (VRF) Systems: VRF systems provide simultaneous heating and cooling to different zones within a building, offering flexibility, energy efficiency, and individualized comfort control.

4. Geothermal Heat Pumps: Geothermal Air-conditioning systems harness the stable temperature of the earth to provide efficient heating and cooling, offering long-term energy savings and environmental benefits.

5. Ductless Mini-Split Systems: Ductless mini-split systems offer flexible, zone-based heating and cooling solutions for residential and commercial spaces without ductwork, enhancing energy efficiency and indoor comfort.

Looking ahead, future developments in Air-conditioning technology will focus on integrating renewable energy, enhancing energy efficiency, improving indoor air quality, and embracing smart building technologies to create healthier, more sustainable indoor environments for occupants worldwide.

In conclusion, Air-conditioning technology plays a vital role in maintaining human comfort, health, and productivity by regulating indoor environmental conditions. As the world faces evolving challenges related to climate change, energy consumption, and indoor air quality, innovative solutions and advancements in Air-conditioning technology will be crucial for creating sustainable, resilient indoor spaces that promote the well-being of occupants and the planet.

Exploring Spirituality: The Essence of Human Existence

Spirituality is a multifaceted concept that encompasses the exploration of the deeper dimensions of human existence, the quest for meaning and purpose, and the connection to something greater than oneself. While spirituality is often associated with religion, it extends beyond religious beliefs and rituals to encompass a broader sense of connection to the universe, nature, and the divine.

At its core, spirituality is about awakening to the intrinsic wisdom and interconnectedness of all life, transcending the limitations of the egoic mind, and aligning with the timeless truths that underlie existence. It involves a journey of self-discovery, inner exploration, and transformation, leading to greater awareness, compassion, and fulfillment.

The Importance of Spirituality in Human Life

Spirituality holds profound significance for human life in several ways:

1. Meaning and Purpose: Spirituality provides a framework for understanding the deeper meaning and purpose of life, helping individuals navigate existential questions and find direction in their journey.

2. Inner Peace and Fulfillment: By cultivating a sense of connection to something greater than oneself, spirituality offers a source of inner peace, fulfillment, and resilience amidst life's challenges and uncertainties.

3. Connection and Unity: Spirituality fosters a sense of interconnectedness and unity with all beings, transcending divisions of race, religion, and culture and promoting harmony and compassion in human relationships.

4. Health and Well-being: Numerous studies have shown that spiritual practices such as mindfulness, meditation, and prayer have positive effects on mental, emotional, and physical health,

reducing stress, anxiety, and depression while enhancing overall well-being.

5. Ethical and Moral Values: Spirituality often emphasizes ethical and moral values such as compassion, empathy, and kindness, guiding individuals towards actions that contribute to the greater good of humanity and the planet.

The Deep Connection of Mindfulness, Breathing, and Peace to Human Life

Mindfulness, breathing practices, and inner peace are integral components of spiritual exploration and personal growth, offering profound benefits to human life:

1. Mindfulness: Mindfulness involves paying attention to the present moment with openness, curiosity, and non-judgmental awareness. Through mindfulness practices such as meditation, mindful movement, and conscious living, individuals cultivate greater clarity, presence, and insight, enabling them to respond to life's challenges with equanimity and grace.

2. Breathing: Breathing is not only essential for physical survival but also serves as a bridge between the body and the mind, the conscious and the unconscious. Conscious breathing practices such as pranayama in yoga, qigong in Chinese medicine, and deep diaphragmatic breathing techniques facilitate relaxation, stress reduction, and the cultivation of vital life force energy (prana, chi), promoting holistic health and well-being.

3. Peace: Inner peace is a state of harmony and serenity that arises from a deep sense of connection to oneself, others, and the universe. Through spiritual practices such as meditation, contemplation, and self-inquiry, individuals access the inner reservoir of peace that lies within, transcending the restless fluctuations of the mind and finding refuge in the timeless sanctuary of the heart.

The Future Impact of Spiritual Practices in the Ongoing Life Cycle

As humanity continues to navigate the complexities of the modern world, spiritual practices are poised to play an increasingly significant role in shaping the future of human life:

1. Holistic Well-being: With rising awareness of the interconnectedness of mind, body, and spirit, there is a growing recognition of the importance of holistic approaches to health and

well-being that integrate spiritual practices alongside conventional medical interventions.

2. Resilience and Adaptability: In a rapidly changing world marked by uncertainty and upheaval, spiritual practices offer tools and resources for building resilience, fostering adaptability, and navigating life's transitions with grace and resilience.

3. Social and Environmental Consciousness: Spirituality encourages a sense of responsibility and stewardship towards the planet and all its inhabitants, inspiring individuals to adopt sustainable lifestyle choices, cultivate compassion for others, and contribute to the collective well-being of humanity and the earth.

4. Global Unity and Cooperation: As humanity grapples with pressing global challenges such as climate change, social inequality, and conflict, spirituality fosters a sense of global unity and cooperation, transcending divisions and promoting collaboration towards shared goals of peace, justice, and sustainability.

Embracing a Better Way of Life with Right Spiritual Practices

Embracing spiritual practices offers a pathway to a better way of life characterized by greater meaning, purpose, and fulfillment:

1. Self-Discovery and Authenticity: Spiritual practices invite individuals to explore the depths of their being, uncovering their

true essence and aligning with their authentic selves, leading to greater self-awareness, self-acceptance, and self-expression.

2. Compassionate Action: Rooted in love and compassion, spiritual practices inspire individuals to engage in acts of kindness, service, and generosity towards others, fostering a culture of empathy, understanding, and mutual support.

3. Harmony with Nature: Spirituality fosters a deep reverence for the natural world and a recognition of humanity's interconnectedness with all living beings. By embracing ecological principles and living in harmony with nature, individuals cultivate a sustainable way of life that honors the earth and its ecosystems.

4. Inner Peace and Equanimity: Through spiritual practices such as meditation, mindfulness, and contemplation, individuals cultivate inner peace, equanimity, and resilience, enabling them to navigate life's challenges with grace and serenity.

In conclusion, spirituality offers a profound pathway to deeper meaning, connection, and fulfillment in human life. By embracing spiritual practices such as mindfulness,

breathing, and inner peace, individuals can awaken to the inherent wisdom and interconnectedness of all existence, leading to greater well-being, harmony, and compassion for oneself, others, and the world. As humanity continues its ongoing life cycle, the integration of spiritual principles and practices holds the potential to create a more enlightened, compassionate, and sustainable future for all.

Exploring the Common Ground Between Air-conditioning and Spirituality in Human Comfort

Human comfort is a fundamental aspect of both Air-conditioning (Heating, Ventilation, and Air Conditioning) systems and spirituality. While they may seem unrelated at first glance, there are profound connections between the two when it comes to enhancing human well-being and comfort. In this comprehensive exploration, we'll delve into the common ground shared by

Air-conditioning and spirituality in facilitating human comfort, addressing physical, emotional, and spiritual aspects of well-being.

1. Regulation of Temperature and Emotional Equilibrium:

At its core, Air-conditioning systems are designed to regulate indoor temperatures to ensure occupants' comfort. Similarly, spirituality offers tools and practices to regulate emotional states and cultivate inner equilibrium. Just as Air-conditioning systems adjust temperatures to maintain a comfortable environment, spiritual practices such as mindfulness, meditation, and breathwork help individuals regulate emotional responses, manage stress, and find inner balance amidst life's fluctuations.

2. Optimization of Air Quality and Inner Clarity:

Air-conditioning systems play a crucial role in optimizing indoor air quality by filtering out pollutants and allergens, promoting healthier living environments. Similarly, spiritual practices contribute to inner clarity and purification, removing mental and emotional pollutants that cloud the mind and hinder personal growth. Through practices like meditation and self-reflection, individuals cleanse the mind of negativity and cultivate clarity, enhancing mental well-being and cognitive function.

3. Creation of Sacred Spaces and Inner Sanctuary:

Air-conditioning systems create comfortable indoor environments that serve as physical sanctuaries for relaxation and rejuvenation. Likewise, spirituality invites individuals to create sacred spaces within themselves, where they can retreat from the chaos of the external world and connect with their innermost essence. Through practices like meditation, prayer, and ritual, individuals cultivate inner sanctuaries of peace and tranquility, nourishing the soul and replenishing the spirit.

4. Promotion of Energy Efficiency and Vitality:

Air-conditioning systems strive for energy efficiency to minimize waste and optimize performance, promoting sustainability and cost-effectiveness. Similarly, spiritual practices aim to optimize the flow of energy within the body, mind, and spirit, enhancing vitality and well-being. Practices like yoga, qigong, and tai chi stimulate the body's energy channels (prana, chi) and promote holistic health, vitality, and longevity.

5. Integration of Smart Technology and Higher Wisdom:

Modern Air-conditioning systems leverage smart technology and automation to enhance efficiency, comfort, and convenience for occupants. Similarly, spirituality integrates higher wisdom and divine guidance to optimize human well-being and fulfillment. Through spiritual practices and teachings, individuals access innate wisdom and intuition, guiding them towards choices and actions aligned with their highest good and purpose.

6. Adaptation to Changing Conditions and Resilience:

Air-conditioning systems are designed to adapt to changing environmental conditions to maintain optimal comfort for occupants. Likewise, spirituality fosters resilience and adaptability in individuals, enabling them to navigate life's challenges and uncertainties with grace and fortitude. Spiritual practices cultivate inner strength, flexibility, and acceptance, empowering individuals to weather life's storms and emerge stronger and wiser.

7. Cultivation of Harmony and Unity:

Air-conditioning systems create harmonious indoor environments where occupants can thrive and coexist in comfort and harmony. Similarly, spirituality fosters unity and interconnectedness among individuals, transcending differences and promoting compassion, empathy, and cooperation. Through spiritual practices, individuals cultivate a sense of oneness with all beings and the universe, fostering peace, understanding, and mutual respect.

Conclusion:

In conclusion, the connections between Air-conditioning and spirituality in facilitating human comfort are profound and multifaceted. Both aim to create environments that nurture physical, emotional, and spiritual well-being, promoting harmony, balance, and vitality for individuals and communities. By recognizing the common ground shared by Air-conditioning systems and spirituality, we can harness the synergies between the two to create environments that support holistic human flourishing and contribute to a more sustainable and compassionate world.

In spirituality, breathing serves as a central focal point, representing the fundamental connection between the physical body and the deeper realms of consciousness. Similarly, in Air-conditioning systems, the compressor plays a crucial role as the heart of the system, responsible for circulating refrigerant and regulating temperature. Despite their apparent differences, both breathing and the compressor share striking parallels in their roles and impacts on human comfort and well-being.

Breathing in Spirituality:

Breathing is more than just a physiological function; it serves as a gateway to the inner realms of consciousness and a tool for cultivating mindfulness, presence, and spiritual awareness. In many spiritual traditions, conscious breathing practices are integral to meditation, yoga, and other contemplative practices, facilitating relaxation, inner peace, and spiritual growth.

Role of Breathing:

1. Connection to the Present Moment: Conscious breathing anchors individuals in the present moment, allowing them to

release the grip of past regrets and future anxieties, and fully engage with the richness of life unfolding in the here and now.

2. Integration of Mind and Body: Breathing bridges the gap between the mind and body, serving as a conduit for the flow of vital life force energy (prana, chi). Through conscious breathing, individuals harmonize their physical, emotional, and spiritual dimensions, promoting holistic well-being and integration.

3. Expansion of Consciousness: Deep, rhythmic breathing patterns expand awareness and facilitate shifts in consciousness, opening the door to transcendent states of unity, insight, and transcendence. In these altered states, individuals may experience profound insights, spiritual revelations, and a deep sense of connection to the divine.

Impact of Breathing Practices:

1. Stress Reduction and Relaxation: Conscious breathing practices induce the relaxation response, activating the parasympathetic nervous system and counteracting the physiological effects of stress. By cultivating a state of relaxation and calm, breathing practices promote emotional balance, mental clarity, and overall well-being.

2. Enhanced Mindfulness and Presence: Conscious breathing fosters mindfulness and presence, enabling individuals to cultivate non-judgmental awareness of their thoughts, emotions, and sensations. Through mindful breathing, individuals develop

greater clarity, focus, and insight into the nature of their inner experience.

3. Spiritual Awakening and Transformation: Conscious breathing serves as a catalyst for spiritual awakening and transformation, catalyzing profound shifts in consciousness and perception. By exploring the depths of their breath, individuals may uncover dormant aspects of themselves, release unconscious patterns, and awaken to higher states of consciousness.

The Compressor in Air-conditioning Systems:

The compressor serves as the heart of Air-conditioning systems, responsible for pressurizing and circulating refrigerant to facilitate

the cooling or heating process. It plays a pivotal role in regulating temperature and maintaining comfort levels within indoor environments.

Role of the Compressor:

1. Temperature Regulation: The compressor cycles refrigerant between high and low-pressure states, facilitating the transfer of heat from indoor spaces to the exterior during cooling mode and vice versa during heating mode. By compressing and expanding refrigerant gases, the compressor regulates indoor temperatures to ensure optimal comfort for occupants.

2. Efficiency and Performance: The compressor's efficiency directly impacts the performance and energy consumption of Air-conditioning systems. Modern compressors are designed for maximum efficiency, utilizing advanced technologies such as variable-speed drives and scroll or rotary compressors to optimize energy usage and minimize operational costs.

3. Reliability and Durability: The reliability and durability of Air-conditioning systems depend on the quality and performance of the compressor. Well-maintained compressors ensure consistent operation and longevity, minimizing downtime and maintenance requirements for Air-conditioning systems.

Impact of the Compressor:

1. Comfort and Climate Control: The compressor's role in regulating temperature directly impacts occupants' comfort and well-being within indoor environments. By maintaining stable temperatures, the compressor creates a comfortable living or working environment conducive to productivity, relaxation, and overall satisfaction.

2. Energy Efficiency and Sustainability: Efficient compressors contribute to energy savings and environmental sustainability by reducing electricity consumption and greenhouse gas emissions associated with Air-conditioning operation. By investing in high-efficiency compressors, building owners and operators can lower operational costs and minimize their carbon footprint.

3. System Performance and Reliability: The performance and reliability of Air-conditioning systems hinge on the compressor's ability to maintain consistent operation under varying load conditions. Properly sized and maintained compressors ensure reliable performance, optimal comfort, and longevity for Air-conditioning systems, enhancing occupants' quality of life and satisfaction.

Synthesis of Breathing and Compressor Roles:

Despite their apparent differences, breathing and the compressor share fundamental similarities in their roles and impacts on human comfort and well-being. Both serve as essential mechanisms for regulating temperature, energy flow, and vitality within their respective domains—whether it be the internal landscape of consciousness or the external environment of indoor spaces.

Parallel Impacts on Comfort and Well-being:

1. Regulation of Temperature: Just as conscious breathing regulates internal temperature and energy flow within the body, the compressor regulates temperature and energy flow within indoor environments, ensuring optimal comfort and climate control for occupants.

2. Enhancement of Efficiency: Both breathing practices and efficient compressors promote energy efficiency and sustainability, minimizing waste and maximizing the utilization of available resources to support human comfort and well-being.

3. Promotion of Relaxation and Resilience: Conscious breathing practices and reliable compressors contribute to relaxation, resilience, and well-being by fostering a sense of stability, equilibrium, and ease within individuals and indoor environments.

In essence, the parallels between breathing and the compressor underscore the interconnectedness of physical, emotional, and spiritual dimensions of human experience. By recognizing and harnessing the synergy between these seemingly disparate elements, individuals and communities can cultivate environments that promote holistic well-being, comfort, and vitality for all.

In Vedic science, spirituality encompasses a profound understanding of the interconnectedness of all existence and the quest for self-realization and union with the divine. Rooted in ancient wisdom and scriptures such as the Vedas and the Bhagavad Gita, spirituality in Vedic tradition offers a holistic framework for living a meaningful and fulfilling life. Let's explore how spirituality is defined in Vedic science, astrology, and the Vedas, and delve into the essential teachings of the Bhagavad Gita for all human beings.

1. Spirituality in Vedic Science:

In Vedic science, spirituality is the journey of self-discovery and inner transformation, leading to the realization of one's true nature and ultimate purpose. Central to Vedic spirituality is the concept of "Atman," the eternal, unchanging essence of the individual that is inherently connected to the universal consciousness or "Brahman." Through practices such as meditation, yoga, and self-inquiry, individuals seek to transcend the limitations of the egoic mind and align with the higher truths of existence.

Vedic spirituality emphasizes the interconnectedness of all life forms and the sacredness of the natural world. It recognizes the divinity inherent in every being and encourages reverence for the earth, the elements, and the cosmos. By honoring this interconnectedness and living in harmony with the rhythms of nature, individuals cultivate a deep sense of peace, fulfillment, and spiritual attunement.

2. Spirituality in Astrology:

In Vedic astrology, spirituality plays a significant role in guiding individuals towards self-awareness, personal growth, and alignment with cosmic forces. Astrology is seen as a tool for understanding the soul's journey through lifetimes and uncovering karmic patterns and soul lessons. By studying the positions of the planets and their influence on human consciousness and destiny, individuals gain insights into their spiritual path and evolution.

Astrology encourages individuals to recognize their innate strengths, weaknesses, and soul purpose, empowering them to make conscious choices and navigate life's challenges with wisdom and resilience. Through practices such as jyotish meditation and mantra recitation, individuals can align with the cosmic energies and cultivate spiritual awareness, balance, and harmony in their lives.

3. Spirituality in the Vedas:

The Vedas, the ancient scriptures of India, form the foundation of Vedic spirituality and contain timeless wisdom and teachings about the nature of reality, the purpose of life, and the path to spiritual liberation. The Vedas emphasize the importance of self-discipline, moral conduct, and devotion to the divine as essential aspects of spiritual practice.

One of the most revered texts in the Vedic tradition is the Bhagavad Gita, a sacred dialogue between Lord Krishna and the warrior prince Arjuna, which offers profound insights into the nature of the self, the principles of dharma (righteousness), and the path to spiritual enlightenment. The Bhagavad Gita teaches that true spirituality lies in the performance of one's duty (svadharma) with devotion and detachment, surrendering the fruits of one's actions to the divine.

Essential Teachings of the Bhagavad Gita:

The Bhagavad Gita offers timeless wisdom and practical guidance for all human beings on their spiritual journey. Some of its key teachings include:

1. Dharma and Karma: The Gita emphasizes the importance of fulfilling one's duty (dharma) with integrity and devotion, regardless of the outcomes or consequences (karma). By aligning with one's inherent nature and responsibilities, individuals can live a life of purpose and fulfillment.

2. Detachment and Renunciation: While encouraging active engagement in the world, the Gita also teaches the importance of detachment and renunciation of attachment to the fruits of one's actions. By cultivating equanimity and surrendering personal desires and expectations, individuals can attain inner peace and freedom from suffering.

3. Yoga and Self-Realization: The Gita outlines various paths of yoga, including karma yoga (the yoga of selfless action), bhakti yoga (the yoga of devotion), and jnana yoga (the yoga of knowledge), as means of attaining self-realization and union with the divine. By practicing these paths with sincerity and dedication, individuals can transcend the limitations of the ego and experience the ultimate reality of Brahman.

4. Unity of All Existence: At its core, the Bhagavad Gita teaches the essential unity of all existence and the underlying oneness of the universe. By recognizing the divinity within oneself and all beings, individuals can cultivate compassion, empathy, and reverence for all life forms, fostering harmony and peace in the world.

Conclusion:

In Vedic science, astrology, and the Vedas, spirituality is the journey of self-discovery, inner transformation, and union with the divine. Rooted in ancient wisdom and teachings, spirituality offers a holistic framework for living a meaningful and fulfilling life, guiding individuals towards self-awareness, personal growth, and alignment with cosmic forces. The Bhagavad Gita, in particular, offers profound insights into the nature of reality, the principles of righteousness, and the path to spiritual enlightenment, serving as a timeless guide for all human beings on their spiritual journey. By embracing the teachings of Vedic spirituality and the Bhagavad Gita, individuals can cultivate inner peace, fulfillment, and harmony, and contribute to the creation of a more enlightened and compassionate world.

The Evolution of Air-conditioning: From Inception to Future Innovations

The advent of Heating, Ventilation, and Air Conditioning (Air-conditioning) systems has revolutionized the way we live and work, providing essential comfort and environmental control in various settings. Understanding the origins of Air-conditioning, its technological evolution over the past century, and its future trajectory is crucial for appreciating its impact on human life and well-being.

1. Origins and Early Development:

The concept of environmental control dates back centuries, with ancient civilizations employing various methods to regulate indoor temperatures and air quality. However, the modern Air-conditioning system as we know it today emerged in the late 19th and early 20th centuries with the invention of air conditioning and refrigeration technologies.

One of the key pioneers in the development of air conditioning systems was Willis Carrier, an American engineer who invented the first modern air conditioner in 1902. Carrier's invention, initially designed to control humidity in a printing plant, laid the foundation for modern Air-conditioning systems by introducing the principles of refrigeration and air cooling.

2. Technological Advances in the Past Decade:

Over the past decade, Air-conditioning technology has undergone significant advancements driven by a growing emphasis on energy efficiency, sustainability, and user comfort. Some notable developments include:

a. Energy-Efficient Systems: The introduction of high-efficiency Air-conditioning systems, including variable-speed compressors, advanced controls, and variable refrigerant flow (VRF) technology, has led to significant energy savings and reduced environmental impact.

b. Smart Air-conditioning Controls: The integration of smart technology and IoT (Internet of Things) connectivity has enabled the development of intelligent Air-conditioning systems capable of remote monitoring, predictive maintenance, and adaptive temperature control, enhancing user comfort and operational efficiency.

c. Sustainable Solutions: The adoption of renewable energy sources such as solar power, geothermal heat pumps, and biomass heating systems has emerged as a sustainable alternative to traditional Air-conditioning systems, reducing reliance on fossil fuels and mitigating greenhouse gas emissions.

d. Air Quality Enhancement: Growing concerns about indoor air quality and health have led to advancements in air filtration, purification, and ventilation technologies, including the use of HEPA filters, UV-C light, and energy recovery ventilation (ERV) systems to remove pollutants and allergens and promote healthier indoor environments.

3. Future Trends and Innovations:

Looking ahead, the future of Air-conditioning technology is characterized by several key trends and innovations aimed at enhancing comfort, efficiency, and sustainability:

a. Zero-Energy Buildings: The development of net-zero energy buildings, which produce as much energy as they consume, is driving demand for ultra-efficient Air-conditioning systems, advanced building envelopes, and integrated renewable energy solutions to minimize energy consumption and environmental impact.

b. Artificial Intelligence (AI) Integration: AI-powered Air-conditioning systems equipped with machine learning algorithms and predictive analytics capabilities will enable autonomous operation, adaptive temperature control, and proactive maintenance, optimizing performance and energy efficiency.

c. Climate-Responsive Design: With climate change posing unprecedented challenges, climate-responsive Air-conditioning design strategies, including passive cooling techniques, natural ventilation, and thermal mass, will become increasingly important for mitigating heat stress and reducing energy consumption in buildings.

d. Health-Centric Solutions: The COVID-19 pandemic has heightened awareness of indoor air quality and health, driving demand for Air-conditioning solutions that prioritize air filtration, purification, and humidity control to reduce the spread of airborne pathogens and improve occupant comfort and well-being.

4. Necessity of Air-conditioning in Human Life:

The role of Air-conditioning in human life cannot be overstated, particularly in regions with extreme climates or densely populated urban areas. Air-conditioning systems provide essential comfort, safety, and productivity in various settings, including:

a. Residential Spaces: Air-conditioning systems create comfortable indoor environments for homeowners, ensuring thermal comfort, air quality, and humidity control year-round. Without Air-conditioning, individuals would be vulnerable to temperature extremes, allergens, and indoor pollutants, compromising their health and well-being.

b. Commercial Buildings: Air-conditioning systems play a critical role in commercial settings such as offices, retail stores, and healthcare facilities, where occupant comfort, productivity, and customer satisfaction are paramount. Efficient Air-conditioning systems also contribute to employee retention, customer loyalty, and business success.

c. Industrial Facilities: In industrial settings, Air-conditioning systems are essential for maintaining optimal conditions for manufacturing processes, equipment operation, and worker safety. Proper ventilation, temperature control, and humidity regulation are crucial for preventing equipment malfunctions, product defects, and heat-related injuries.

d. Transportation: Air-conditioning systems are integral components of vehicles, aircraft, trains, and ships, providing climate control and passenger comfort during travel. Without Air-conditioning, passengers would be exposed to uncomfortable temperatures, poor air quality, and increased risk of heatstroke or hypothermia.

5. Life Without Air-conditioning:

Imagine a world without Air-conditioning—where indoor temperatures fluctuate wildly with the weather, air quality is compromised by pollutants and allergens, and comfort is a luxury reserved for the privileged few. In such a world, individuals would struggle to cope with extreme heat or cold, leading to discomfort, stress, and health issues.

Without Air-conditioning, productivity would decline in workplaces, students would struggle to focus in classrooms, and patients would suffer in healthcare facilities. Residential dwellings would become inhospitable environments, with families enduring sweltering summers and freezing winters, unable to escape the elements.

In summary, Air-conditioning technology has transformed the way we live, work, and interact with our environment, providing essential comfort, safety, and well-being in a world characterized by diverse climates and urbanization. As we look to the future, continued advancements in Air-conditioning technology will play a crucial role in creating sustainable, resilient, and healthy indoor environments for generations to come.

Aligning Air-conditioning and Spirituality: Finding Common Ground in Modern Life

In our modern lives, it's easy to see Air-conditioning (Heating, Ventilation, and Air Conditioning) systems and spirituality as unrelated or even opposing forces. However, upon closer examination, we can discover profound parallels and commonalities between these seemingly disparate aspects of human existence. By aligning Air-conditioning and spirituality, we can explore how they intersect in shaping our lifestyles, understanding their impact on our well-being, and envisioning a harmonious future that integrates both aspects seamlessly. Let's delve into the common factors, present influences, and future implications of aligning Air-conditioning and spirituality in modern life.

1. Comfort and Well-being:

Both Air-conditioning and spirituality are ultimately concerned with promoting comfort and well-being, albeit in different ways. Air-conditioning systems regulate indoor environments to ensure physical comfort, maintaining optimal temperature, humidity levels, and air quality. On the other hand, spirituality addresses emotional, mental, and spiritual well-being, offering practices and teachings that cultivate inner peace, fulfillment, and harmony. By aligning Air-conditioning and spirituality, we can recognize the importance of both physical and spiritual comfort in enhancing overall quality of life.

2. Connection to Nature:

Air-conditioning systems interact with the natural environment, utilizing natural elements such as air, water, and sunlight to create comfortable indoor spaces. Similarly, spirituality emphasizes the interconnectedness of all life and the importance of living in harmony with nature. By recognizing and honoring our connection to the natural world, we can integrate sustainable Air-conditioning practices with spiritual values such as reverence for the earth, conservation of resources, and environmental stewardship.

3. Mindful Living:

Mindfulness is a central theme in both Air-conditioning and spirituality, albeit in different contexts. Air-conditioning systems require careful attention and maintenance to ensure optimal performance and energy efficiency. Similarly, spirituality encourages mindfulness in daily life, promoting present-moment awareness, conscious living, and intentional action. By practicing mindfulness in our interactions with Air-conditioning systems and in our spiritual practices, we can cultivate greater awareness, appreciation, and gratitude for the blessings of modern technology and the gifts of the present moment.

4. Energy Flow and Balance:

Both Air-conditioning and spirituality involve the concept of energy flow and balance, albeit on different levels. Air-conditioning systems regulate the flow of thermal energy to maintain comfortable indoor environments, while spirituality addresses the flow of subtle energies within the body, mind, and spirit. By aligning Air-conditioning practices with spiritual principles such as energy conservation, optimization, and harmonization, we can create environments that promote physical comfort and energetic balance, supporting holistic well-being on all levels.

Present Influences and Future Implications:

In our present-day world, the alignment of Air-conditioning and spirituality is becoming increasingly relevant as we grapple with pressing global challenges such as climate change, environmental degradation, and social inequality. The impact of Air-conditioning systems on the environment and human health has prompted a growing awareness of the need for sustainable Air-conditioning practices and technologies that minimize energy consumption, reduce carbon emissions, and prioritize indoor air quality.

Similarly, the rise of spirituality as a guiding force in modern life reflects a growing recognition of the interconnectedness of all existence and the importance of living in harmony with ourselves, others, and the planet. As individuals and communities embrace spiritual values such as compassion, empathy, and mindfulness, they are increasingly seeking ways to integrate these principles into all aspects of life, including the built environment.

Looking ahead, the alignment of Air-conditioning and spirituality has significant implications for the future of architecture, urban planning, and sustainable development. By integrating green building practices with spiritual values such as simplicity, mindfulness, and interconnectedness, we can create environments that support human well-being, foster ecological harmony, and promote social justice.

In conclusion, aligning Air-conditioning and spirituality offers a holistic approach to modern living that integrates physical comfort with emotional, mental, and spiritual well-being. By recognizing the common factors and shared values between Air-conditioning and spirituality, we can cultivate environments that promote balance, harmony, and sustainability for ourselves, future generations, and the planet as a whole. As we navigate the complexities of the modern world, let us embrace the synergy between technology and spirituality to create a future that honors the interconnectedness of all life and fosters a culture of compassion, mindfulness, and reverence for the earth.

Certainly! Let's delve into some of the best techniques of breathing, yoga, and mantras for mindfulness and spiritual effects.

Breathing Techniques:

1. Diaphragmatic Breathing (Deep Breathing): This technique involves breathing deeply into the diaphragm, allowing the abdomen to rise and fall with each breath. To practice diaphragmatic breathing, sit or lie down in a comfortable position. Place one hand on your abdomen and the other on your chest. Inhale deeply through your nose, allowing your abdomen to rise as you fill your lungs with air. Exhale slowly through your mouth, feeling your abdomen fall. Repeat this process for several minutes, focusing on the sensation of breathing deeply and fully.

2. Alternate Nostril Breathing (Nadi Shodhana): This pranayama technique balances the flow of energy in the body and calms the mind. Sit in a comfortable position with your spine straight. Close your right nostril with your right thumb and inhale deeply through your left nostril. Then, close your left nostril with your ring finger and exhale through your right nostril. Inhale through your right nostril, then close it and exhale through your left nostril. Continue this alternate nostril breathing pattern for several rounds, focusing on the rhythm of your breath.

3. Box Breathing (Square Breathing): This technique helps regulate the breath and promote relaxation. Start by exhaling completely, then inhale deeply for a count of four seconds. Hold

your breath for four seconds, then exhale slowly for four seconds. Hold your breath again for four seconds before inhaling again. Repeat this box breathing pattern for several rounds, focusing on the even rhythm of your breath and the sensations in your body.

Yoga Practices:

1. Sun Salutations (Surya Namaskar): Sun salutations are a sequence of yoga poses that warm up the body, stretch the muscles, and synchronize breath with movement. Begin by standing at the front of your mat with your feet together. Inhale as you raise your arms overhead, then exhale as you fold forward into a forward bend. Inhale to lift your chest into a half forward bend, then exhale to step or jump back into a plank pose. Continue through a series of poses, including downward-facing dog, upward-facing dog, and child's pose. Flow through the sequence with your breath, repeating several rounds to build heat and energy in the body.

2. Mindful Movement (Vinyasa Flow): Vinyasa yoga involves flowing through a series of poses with breath awareness, creating a moving meditation. Begin in a seated or standing position, and inhale as you reach your arms overhead. Exhale as you fold forward into a forward bend, then inhale to lengthen your spine into a half forward bend. Exhale to step or jump back into a plank pose, then lower down through a chaturanga. Inhale to upward-facing dog, then exhale to downward-facing dog. Flow through the sequence with smooth, mindful movements, linking breath with movement and focusing on the present moment.

3. Yoga Nidra (Yogic Sleep): Yoga nidra is a guided meditation practice that induces deep relaxation and promotes spiritual insight. Lie down in savasana (corpse pose) with your arms at your sides and your palms facing up. Close your eyes and focus on your breath, allowing your body to relax completely. The instructor will guide you through a series of visualizations, body scans, and affirmations to promote relaxation and inner awareness. Practice yoga nidra regularly to reduce stress, enhance creativity, and cultivate a deeper connection to your inner self.

Mantras and Affirmations:

1. Om Mantra: The Om mantra is considered the most sacred sound in Hinduism and is often chanted at the beginning and end of yoga classes to invoke a sense of peace and unity. Sit comfortably with your eyes closed and take a few deep breaths to center yourself. Then, chant the sound "Om" aloud or silently, feeling the vibration resonate throughout your body. Repeat the mantra several times, allowing it to quiet the mind and awaken your spiritual consciousness.

2. So Hum Mantra: The So Hum mantra means "I am that" in Sanskrit and is often used as a meditation mantra to cultivate self-awareness and connection to the universe. Sit in a comfortable position with your eyes closed and take a few deep breaths to relax. With each inhale, silently repeat the sound "So," and with each exhale, silently repeat the sound "Hum." Focus on the rhythm of

your breath and the repetition of the mantra, allowing it to deepen your sense of inner peace and unity with all of creation.

3. Affirmations for Self-Love and Empowerment: Affirmations are positive statements that you repeat to yourself to reprogram your subconscious mind and cultivate a positive mindset. Choose affirmations that resonate with you, such as "I am worthy of love and happiness," "I trust in the wisdom of the universe," or "I am capable of achieving my dreams." Repeat your chosen affirmations daily, either silently or aloud, and allow them to uplift your spirits and empower you to live your best life.

Incorporating

These breathing techniques, yoga practices, and mantras into your daily routine can enhance mindfulness, promote relaxation, and deepen your spiritual connection. Whether you're seeking stress relief, inner peace, or spiritual growth, these powerful tools can support you on your journey toward greater well-being and fulfillment. Practice regularly, with intention and dedication, and allow yourself to experience the transformative effects of mindfulness and spirituality in your life.

Improving efficiency in Air-conditioning (Heating, Ventilation, and Air Conditioning) systems is essential for reducing energy consumption, lowering operating costs, and minimizing environmental impact. With a focus on futuristic views and requirements, advancements in Air-conditioning technology aim to enhance efficiency while meeting evolving demands for comfort, sustainability, and performance. Let's explore various strategies and innovations to improve efficiency in Air-conditioning systems for the future.

1. Energy-Efficient Equipment:

Investing in energy-efficient Air-conditioning equipment is a fundamental step towards improving system efficiency. Advancements in technology have led to the development of high-efficiency heating and cooling units, such as variable-speed compressors, modulating gas furnaces, and heat pumps with variable refrigerant flow (VRF) systems. These systems adjust their output based on real-time demand, optimizing energy usage and reducing wastage.

2. Smart Controls and Automation:

Integrating smart controls and automation into Air-conditioning systems enhances efficiency by optimizing operation based on occupancy schedules, weather conditions, and indoor air quality. Smart Spiritual Conditionings, building management systems (BMS), and Internet of Things (IoT) devices enable remote monitoring, predictive maintenance, and adaptive control strategies. These technologies optimize energy usage, improve comfort, and extend equipment lifespan.

3. Energy Recovery Ventilation (ERV) Systems:

Energy recovery ventilation (ERV) systems capture and transfer heat or coolness from exhaust air to incoming fresh air, minimizing energy losses and reducing the workload on heating and cooling equipment. By recovering energy from exhaust air streams, ERV systems pre-condition incoming air, reducing the need for additional heating or cooling and improving overall system efficiency.

4. Advanced Air Filtration and Purification:

Enhancing air filtration and purification capabilities improves indoor air quality while maintaining system efficiency.

High-efficiency particulate air (HEPA) filters, ultraviolet germicidal irradiation (UVGI), and photocatalytic oxidation (PCO) systems remove airborne contaminants, allergens, and pathogens, ensuring a healthy and comfortable indoor environment without compromising airflow or system performance.

5. Building Envelope Improvements:

Addressing building envelope issues, such as insulation, air sealing, and window efficiency, reduces heat gain and loss, minimizing the workload on Air-conditioning systems. Energy-efficient building design, including proper insulation, thermal breaks, and reflective roofing materials, enhances thermal comfort, reduces energy consumption, and improves overall system efficiency.

6. Renewable Energy Integration:

Integrating renewable energy sources, such as solar photovoltaic (PV) panels, geothermal heat pumps, and wind turbines, into Air-conditioning systems reduces reliance on fossil fuels and lowers greenhouse gas emissions. By generating clean, renewable energy onsite, buildings can offset energy consumption from traditional Air-conditioning systems, improving efficiency and sustainability while reducing operational costs.

7. Thermal Energy Storage:

Thermal energy storage (TES) systems store excess thermal energy during off-peak hours and release it when needed, reducing peak demand and optimizing Air-conditioning system efficiency. Phase change materials (PCMs), chilled water storage tanks, and ice storage systems enable buildings to shift energy consumption to periods of lower electricity costs, reducing utility bills and enhancing grid stability.

8. Advanced Building Analytics:

Utilizing advanced building analytics and data-driven optimization tools allows for real-time performance monitoring, fault detection, and system optimization. Machine learning algorithms, predictive analytics, and digital twins analyze vast amounts of data to identify inefficiencies, optimize equipment operation, and predict maintenance needs, improving Air-conditioning system efficiency and reliability.

9. Continuous Commissioning and Maintenance:

Implementing continuous commissioning and proactive maintenance programs ensures Air-conditioning systems operate at peak efficiency throughout their lifecycle. Regular equipment inspections, performance testing, and calibration optimize system performance, identify potential issues early, and prevent energy waste, extending equipment lifespan and reducing lifecycle costs.

10. Occupant Engagement and Behavior Modification:

Educating building occupants about energy-saving practices and encouraging behavior modification initiatives, such as adjusting Spiritual Conditioning settings, utilizing natural ventilation, and minimizing unnecessary energy consumption, promotes energy efficiency and fosters a culture of sustainability. Engaging occupants as active participants in energy conservation efforts enhances system efficiency and reduces environmental impact.

In conclusion, improving efficiency in Air-conditioning systems requires a multifaceted approach that integrates technological advancements, sustainable design principles, and proactive maintenance strategies. By embracing innovative solutions and adopting a holistic view of energy management, buildings can optimize performance, enhance comfort, and minimize environmental footprint, paving the way towards a more sustainable and resilient future.

Certainly! Spirituality encompasses a vast array of beliefs, practices, and philosophies, and there are countless books and quotes that offer profound insights into the nature of existence, the human experience, and the pursuit of inner wisdom. Here, I'll share some notable books and quotes from various spiritual traditions that have inspired and guided seekers on their spiritual journeys.

Books:

1. "The Power of Now" by Eckhart Tolle: This groundbreaking book explores the transformative power of living in the present moment and awakening to the deeper dimensions of consciousness. Tolle offers practical teachings and exercises to help readers break free from the grip of the egoic mind and experience the peace and freedom of spiritual awakening.

2. "Autobiography of a Yogi" by Paramahansa Yogananda: This spiritual classic chronicles the life of Paramahansa Yogananda and his journey from a young seeker in India to a renowned spiritual teacher in the West. Filled with inspiring stories, profound insights, and timeless wisdom, this book offers a glimpse into the mystical realms of yoga, meditation, and self-realization.

3. "The Alchemist" by Paulo Coelho: This beloved novel tells the story of Santiago, a shepherd boy on a quest to fulfill his dreams and discover his true purpose in life. Through his journey across the desert, Santiago learns valuable lessons about following his heart, embracing the unknown, and trusting in the guidance of the universe.

4. "Siddhartha" by Hermann Hesse: Set in ancient India, this philosophical novel follows the spiritual journey of Siddhartha, a young Brahmin who sets out to find enlightenment. Along

the way, Siddhartha encounters various teachers, experiences profound insights, and ultimately discovers the path to inner peace and awakening.

5. "The Tao Te Ching" by Lao Tzu: This ancient Chinese text offers profound wisdom and guidance on the principles of Taoism and the art of living in harmony with the Tao, or the Way. Filled with poetic verses and timeless truths, the Tao Te Ching invites readers to embrace simplicity, spontaneity, and naturalness in all aspects of life.

Quotes:

1. "The only way to make sense out of change is to plunge into it, move with it, and join the dance." - Alan Watts

2. "The mind is everything. What you think, you become." - Buddha

3. "Be here now." - Ram Dass

4. "The soul always knows what to do to heal itself. The challenge is to silence the mind." - Caroline Myss

5. "You are not a drop in the ocean. You are the entire ocean in a drop." - Rumi

6. "In the end, just three things matter: How well we have lived, how well we have loved, how well we have learned to let go." - Jack Kornfield

7. "Your task is not to seek for love, but merely to seek and find all the barriers within yourself that you have built against it." - Rumi

8. "The present moment is the only moment available to us, and it is the door to all moments." - Thich Nhat Hanh

9. "You are the universe experiencing itself." - Alan Watts

10. "The journey of a thousand miles begins with a single step." - Lao Tzu

These books and quotes offer timeless wisdom and inspiration for seekers of all paths and traditions. Whether exploring the depths of consciousness, the mysteries of existence, or the beauty of the present moment, they invite readers to embark on a journey of self-discovery, transformation, and spiritual awakening.

In India, several leading Air-conditioning companies play a significant role in providing heating, ventilation, and air conditioning solutions for commercial, industrial, and residential applications. These companies offer a wide range of products, services, and expertise to meet the diverse needs of customers across various sectors. Let's explore some of the top Air-conditioning companies in India and the essential elements, parts, and accessories required in Air-conditioning systems.

Leading Air-conditioning Companies in India:

1. Blue Star Limited: Blue Star is one of the largest Air-conditioning companies in India, offering a comprehensive range of air conditioning, refrigeration, and engineering solutions. The company provides a wide range of products, including central air conditioning systems, ducted split air conditioners, VRF systems, chillers, and packaged air conditioners.

2. Daikin India: Daikin is a global leader in Air-conditioning technology and is known for its innovative and energy-efficient air conditioning solutions. Daikin India offers a wide range of products, including split ACs, VRV systems, ducted units, chillers,

and air purifiers. The company is renowned for its focus on sustainability and environmental responsibility.

3. Voltas Limited: Voltas is a leading provider of air conditioning and refrigeration solutions in India, offering a wide range of products for residential, commercial, and industrial applications. The company's product portfolio includes split ACs, window ACs, cassette ACs, tower ACs, and ductable units, among others.

4. Carrier Airconditioning & Refrigeration Limited: Carrier is a global leader in Air-conditioning technology and is known for its innovative and energy-efficient solutions. In India, Carrier offers a wide range of products, including split ACs, window ACs, ducted split units, VRF systems, and chillers. The company also provides comprehensive Air-conditioning solutions for various sectors, including commercial buildings, hospitals, and data centers.

5. Mitsubishi Electric India: Mitsubishi Electric is a leading provider of Air-conditioning and automation solutions, offering a wide range of products for residential, commercial, and industrial applications. The company's product portfolio includes split ACs, VRF systems, chillers, air purifiers, and ventilation systems. Mitsubishi Electric is known for its advanced technology and reliability.

6 Carrier Midea India Pvt Ltd is a joint venture between Carrier Corporation, a global leader in heating, ventilation, air conditioning, and refrigeration solutions, and Midea Group, a renowned Chinese manufacturer of home appliances and

Air-conditioning products. Established in 2012, Carrier Midea India brings together the expertise and resources of both companies to provide innovative and reliable Air-conditioning solutions for the Indian market.

Carrier Midea India is committed to sustainability and environmental responsibility, incorporating energy-efficient designs, green technologies, and eco-friendly practices into its products and operations. The company strives to minimize carbon footprint, reduce energy consumption, and promote sustainable development through its Air-conditioning solutions.

Essential Elements, Parts, and Accessories in Air-conditioning:

1. Compressor: The compressor is the heart of an Air-conditioning system and is responsible for compressing refrigerant gas to a high pressure and temperature. It plays a crucial role in the cooling process by circulating refrigerant through the system.

2. Condenser: The condenser is a heat exchanger that removes heat from the refrigerant and converts it from a high-pressure gas to a high-pressure liquid. It is typically located outdoors and dissipates heat into the surrounding air.

3. Evaporator Coil: The evaporator coil is another heat exchanger located indoors that absorbs heat from the air inside the building.

As refrigerant flows through the coil, it evaporates and absorbs heat, cooling the air in the process.

4. Expansion Valve: The expansion valve regulates the flow of refrigerant into the evaporator coil, controlling the temperature and pressure of the refrigerant as it enters the coil. It ensures optimal performance and efficiency of the Air-conditioning system.

5. Air Handler: The air handler is a unit that circulates air throughout the Air-conditioning system, distributing cooled or heated air to different parts of the building. It typically contains the evaporator coil, blower fan, and filters.

6. Spiritual Conditioning: The Spiritual Conditioning is a control device that allows users to set and maintain the desired temperature in the building. It communicates with the Air-conditioning system to regulate heating and cooling operations based on the user's preferences.

7. Ductwork: Ductwork consists of a network of pipes or channels that distribute air from the Air-conditioning system to various rooms and spaces within the building. Properly designed and installed ductwork ensures efficient airflow and temperature distribution throughout the building.

8. Filters: Filters are essential components of Air-conditioning systems that remove airborne particles, dust, and pollutants from

the air. They help maintain indoor air quality and protect the system from debris and contaminants.

9. Fans and Blowers: Fans and blowers are used to circulate air through the Air-conditioning system, providing ventilation and ensuring adequate airflow. They can be located in the air handler or in separate units, such as exhaust fans or supply fans.

10. Accessories: Various accessories, such as dampers, grilles, diffusers, and registers, are used to control airflow, direct air distribution, and regulate ventilation in Air-conditioning systems. These components play a crucial role in optimizing system performance and comfort.

In conclusion, the Air-conditioning industry in India is characterized by the presence of several leading companies that offer a wide range of products and solutions for diverse applications. From air conditioning systems and chillers to ventilation equipment and control devices, the essential elements, parts, and accessories in Air-conditioning systems work together to provide efficient and reliable heating, ventilation, and air conditioning for buildings and spaces of all types.

The common message for human life with respect to spirituality and Air-conditioning lies in the understanding of harmony, balance, and interconnectedness. Both realms offer profound insights into the importance of nurturing well-being, fostering sustainability, and cultivating a deeper connection to ourselves, others, and the world around us. Let's explore this common message in detail:

1. Harmony and Balance:

In spirituality, harmony and balance are central principles that guide individuals towards inner peace and alignment with the natural rhythms of life. Through practices such as meditation, yoga, and mindfulness, individuals seek to harmonize their thoughts, emotions, and actions, cultivating a sense of equilibrium and wholeness within themselves.

Similarly, in Air-conditioning, harmony and balance are essential for optimizing system performance and comfort. Air-conditioning systems are designed to regulate temperature, humidity, and air quality to create balanced indoor environments that promote well-being and productivity. By maintaining the right balance of heating, ventilation, and air conditioning, Air-conditioning systems ensure optimal comfort and efficiency while minimizing energy consumption and environmental impact.

2. Interconnectedness and Unity:

Spirituality teaches us that we are all interconnected beings, intimately connected to each other and to the web of life. Through practices of compassion, empathy, and service, individuals recognize the inherent unity of all existence and cultivate a sense of belonging and interconnectedness with the world.

Similarly, Air-conditioning systems operate on the principle of interconnectedness, with various components working together to create comfortable and healthy indoor environments. From the compressor and condenser to the ductwork and ventilation fans, each part of the Air-conditioning system plays a crucial role in maintaining balance and harmony within the built environment. By recognizing the interconnectedness of these components, Air-conditioning professionals can design and operate systems that maximize efficiency and comfort while minimizing waste and inefficiency.

3. Nurturing Well-Being:

At the heart of spirituality is the pursuit of well-being and fulfillment on all levels – physical, emotional, mental, and spiritual. Through practices of self-care, self-awareness, and self-transformation, individuals seek to nurture their holistic well-being and live in alignment with their highest potential.

Similarly, Air-conditioning systems play a vital role in nurturing well-being by creating comfortable, healthy, and safe indoor environments. Proper ventilation, air filtration, and humidity control help maintain indoor air quality and reduce the risk of respiratory problems and other health issues. By prioritizing indoor comfort and wellness, Air-conditioning professionals contribute to the overall well-being and quality of life of building occupants.

4. Sustainability and Stewardship:

Spirituality emphasizes the importance of stewardship and responsibility towards the Earth and all its inhabitants. By living in harmony with nature and practicing sustainable living, individuals honor their interconnectedness with the planet and strive to preserve and protect its resources for future generations.

Similarly, in Air-conditioning, sustainability is a guiding principle that shapes the design, operation, and maintenance of systems. Energy-efficient technologies, renewable energy sources, and green building practices are increasingly being integrated into Air-conditioning solutions to minimize environmental impact and promote sustainability. By embracing sustainable Air-conditioning practices, professionals can reduce energy consumption, lower carbon emissions, and contribute to a more eco-friendly built environment.

Conclusion:

In conclusion, the common message for human life with respect to spirituality and Air-conditioning lies in the recognition of harmony, balance, interconnectedness, well-being, and sustainability. Whether through spiritual practices or Air-conditioning solutions, individuals are invited to cultivate a deeper understanding of themselves, their environment, and their place in the world. By embracing these shared principles and values, we can create spaces and communities that honor the interconnectedness of all life and promote the well-being and flourishing of individuals and the planet as a whole.

Chapter 1

INTRODUCTION - SETTING THE TEMPERATURE OF LIFE

Introduction: The Delicate Balance of Spiritual Conditioning:

In the vast expanse of existence, there exists a delicate balance, much like the delicate equilibrium maintained by a Spiritual Conditioning in an Air-conditioning system. Just as the Spiritual Conditioning regulates the temperature of a room, we too possess an inner mechanism to set the temperature of our lives. This book embarks on a journey to explore the parallels between the functioning of Air-conditioning systems and the intricacies of human spirituality.

Finding Inner Equilibrium: The Core of Spiritual Balance:

At the core of both Air-conditioning systems and human existence lies the concept of balance. Just as an air conditioner adjusts the temperature to ensure comfort, we must strive to find equilibrium in our thoughts, emotions, and actions. Through practices like meditation and mindfulness, we can learn to regulate our internal Spiritual Conditioning, fostering a sense of harmony within ourselves.

Ancient Practices: Inputs to Spiritual Conditioning:

Drawing inspiration from ancient wisdom traditions, we will delve into the teachings of mantras, mudras, and yogic practices to enhance our understanding. Just as a Spiritual Conditioning responds to input signals to maintain the desired temperature, these practices serve as inputs to our consciousness, guiding us towards inner balance and serenity. Let us embark on this journey together, as we uncover the profound connections between Air-conditioning and human spirituality.

CHAPTER 2

THE BREATH OF LIFE - INHALING COLD, EXHALING HEAT

Breath: The Circulating Life Force:

Breath, the essence of life, flows through us like the air circulating through an Air-conditioning system. Just as the compressor draws in air to cool, we inhale the coolness of existence, invigorating our being with each breath. As we exhale, we release the heat of our experiences, allowing it to dissipate into the vast expanse of consciousness.

Pranayama: Regulating the Flow of Energy:

In the practice of pranayama, we harness the power of breath to regulate our internal temperature. Through techniques like alternate nostril breathing, we balance the flow of energy within the body, akin to the regulation of airflow in Air-conditioning systems. With each inhalation, we draw in vitality and rejuvenation; with each exhalation, we release tension and negativity, creating space for inner peace to flourish.

Breath as the Conduit of Energy Exchange:

Just as the coil in an air conditioner facilitates the exchange of hot and cold air, our breath serves as the conduit for the exchange of energy within us. Through mindful breathing, we align ourselves with the natural rhythms of existence, harmonizing with the ebb and flow of life. Let us embrace the transformative power of the breath, as we journey deeper into the realms of spirituality and self-discovery.

CHAPTER 3
FINDING BALANCE - THE THERMOSTAT WITHIN

Spiritual Conditioning: Regulating Inner Equilibrium:

Within each of us resides a Spiritual Conditioning of sorts, capable of regulating the temperature of our inner landscape. Like the Spiritual Conditioning in an Air-conditioning system, this internal mechanism ensures that we remain in a state of equilibrium, neither too hot nor too cold. Through the practices of meditation and mindfulness, we learn to tune into this innate wisdom, guiding us towards balance and harmony.

Self-Awareness: Calibrating Our Inner Guidance System:

Just as the Spiritual Conditioning responds to fluctuations in temperature, our inner guidance system alerts us to imbalances within ourselves. When we veer off course, experiencing extremes of emotion or thought, we can turn inward and recalibrate, much like adjusting the settings on an air conditioner. By cultivating self-awareness and presence, we empower ourselves to navigate life's ever-changing climate with grace and poise.

The Journey of Balance: Yoga and Ayurveda's Teachings:

In the teachings of yoga and Ayurveda, balance is a central tenet, reflecting the interconnectedness of mind, body, and spirit. Through the practice of asanas (postures) and pranayama (breath control), we harmonize the flow of energy within the subtle body, aligning ourselves with the rhythms of the universe. As we embrace the journey towards equilibrium, we discover the true essence of inner peace and fulfillment.

CHAPTER 4

COOLING THE MIND - HARNESSING THE POWER OF CHILL

Cultivating Inner Coolness Amid Life's Heat:

Amidst the heat of life's challenges and stressors, it is essential to cultivate a sense of coolness within the mind. Much like the cooling mechanism of an air conditioner, we can tap into the power of chill to soothe our mental landscape and find respite from the intensity of modern living. Through mindfulness practices and relaxation techniques, we learn to create an inner oasis of calm amidst the chaos.

Shitali Pranayama: Harnessing the Power of Cooling Breath:

In the ancient wisdom traditions of the East, the concept of "shitali pranayama" (cooling breath) is revered for its ability to pacify the mind and body. By inhaling through a curled tongue or pursed lips, we draw in coolness and tranquility, dispersing heat and tension with each breath. This simple yet potent practice serves as a reminder of our innate capacity to find peace within, even in the midst of life's storms.

The Power of Chill: Transforming Heat into Clarity:

As we cultivate a sense of coolness within the mind, we also invite clarity and insight to blossom. Like the condenser in an air conditioner, which transforms hot, gaseous refrigerant into cool, liquid form, we too can transmute the heat of our thoughts into clear, coherent understanding. Through the power of chill, we unlock the gateway to greater self-awareness and wisdom, illuminating the path to inner liberation.

CHAPTER 5

HEATING THE SOUL - IGNITING INNER FIRE

Igniting the Fire of Transformation Within:

Just as heaters warm the air in Air-conditioning systems, we possess the ability to ignite the fire of transformation within our souls. This inner fire, known as "agni" in yoga and Ayurveda, represents the spark of vitality and passion that propels us forward on our spiritual journey. Through practices like meditation, mantra chanting, and visualization, we stoke the flames of our inner furnace, awakening our true potential and purpose.

Agni Sara: Cultivating Inner Heat and Vitality:

In the yogic tradition, the practice of "agni sara" (fire essence) involves engaging the abdominal muscles to generate heat and energy within the body. Much like the heating element of a heater, this technique kindles the fire of digestion and metabolism, fueling

9

our physical and spiritual vitality. As we cultivate the inner heat of transformation, we burn away the layers of conditioning and limitation, revealing the radiant essence of our true nature.

Directing the Flow of Inner Energy Through Intention:

Just as the valves in an Air-conditioning system regulate the flow of heat, our intentions and actions direct the movement of energy within us. By aligning our thoughts, words, and deeds with our highest aspirations, we channel the transformative power of fire into every aspect of our lives. With each conscious choice and heartfelt endeavor, we fan the flames of our inner potential, illuminating the path to self-realization and fulfillment.

CHAPTER 6

ENERGY FLOW - CIRCULATING LIFE FORCE

Prana: The Life Force Energy Within:

Within the intricate network of our being flows the life force energy, known as "prana" in yoga and "chi" in Chinese medicine. Like the circulation of air in Air-conditioning systems, this subtle energy permeates every cell and fiber of our being, sustaining our vitality and vitality. Through practices like yoga, tai chi, and qigong, we learn to harmonize the flow of prana within the body, enhancing our health, and well-being on all levels.

Pranayama: Regulating the Flow of Prana:

In the yogic tradition, the practice of "pranayama" involves conscious control of the breath to regulate the flow of prana within the body. By directing the breath through specific channels, we clear energetic blockages and awaken dormant potential, much like the circulation of air through ducts and vents in Air-conditioning systems. As we attune ourselves to the subtle rhythms of prana, we tap into the boundless reservoir of vitality and creativity that lies within.

Spiritual Practices as Insulation for Prana:

Just as insulation in Air-conditioning systems prevents energy loss and ensures efficient operation, our spiritual practices serve as a protective barrier against the dissipation of prana. Through meditation, mantra chanting, and energy healing, we strengthen our energetic field, shielding ourselves from external influences and maintaining inner balance. As we cultivate resilience and vitality, we become vessels of light and love, radiating our essence into the world with grace and ease.

CHAPTER 7

EFFICIENCY AND OPTIMIZATION - MAXIMIZING POTENTIAL

Efficiency in Personal Growth and Self-Alignment:

Efficiency is the cornerstone of both Air-conditioning systems and personal growth. Just as an air conditioner operates optimally when all its components work in harmony, we too thrive when we align our thoughts, emotions, and actions with our highest potential. Through mindfulness practices and self-reflection, we can identify areas of inefficiency within ourselves and optimize our internal systems for peak performance.

Santosha: Cultivating Contentment for Energy Conservation:

In the yogic tradition, the concept of "santosha" (contentment) encourages us to find satisfaction and fulfillment in the present moment. By cultivating gratitude and acceptance for what is, we minimize energy wastage on futile pursuits and channel our resources towards endeavors that nourish and uplift us. Like the efficient operation of an Air-conditioning system, this attitude of contentment enables us to conserve our vital energy and thrive in all aspects of life.

The Power of Connection in Personal and Collective Growth:

Just as connecting pipes facilitate the smooth flow of refrigerant in Air-conditioning systems, our connections with others play a crucial role in our personal growth and development. By surrounding ourselves with supportive and inspiring individuals, we create an ecosystem of mutual encouragement and growth, much like the interconnected components of a well-designed Air-conditioning system. As we collaborate and co-create with others, we amplify our collective potential and contribute to the greater good of humanity.

CHAPTER 8

FILTERS OF THE MIND – PURIFYING THOUGHTS

Purifying the Mind: Cleansing Mental Filters:

The mind, much like the air passing through filters in Air-conditioning systems, is susceptible to contamination from negative thoughts and emotions. Just as air filters purify the air we breathe, we must purify our minds to maintain clarity and well-being. Through practices like meditation, mindfulness, and self-inquiry, we can cleanse the mental filters of limiting beliefs and conditioned patterns, allowing the pure essence of our true nature to shine forth.

Pratyahara: Withdrawing from External Distractions:

In the yogic tradition, the practice of "pratyahara" (sense withdrawal) involves turning inward and disengaging from external distractions, much like the function of filters in Air-conditioning systems to block out impurities. By withdrawing our attention from the sensory stimuli that agitate the mind, we create space for inner peace and insight to emerge. As we purify the filters of our consciousness, we cultivate a state of clarity and discernment, guiding us towards right action and alignment with our highest truth.

Self-Care and Maintenance for Mental Purity:

Just as regular maintenance ensures the optimal performance of filters in Air-conditioning systems, consistent self-care practices are essential for maintaining the purity of our minds. By prioritizing activities that nourish and uplift us, such as spending time in nature, engaging in creative expression, and connecting with loved ones, we replenish our mental reserves and strengthen our resilience to negativity. As we commit to the ongoing purification of our thoughts, we create a fertile inner landscape for the seeds of positivity and possibility to take root and flourish.

Chapter 9

DUCTS OF DESTINY - NAVIGATING LIFE'S PATHWAYS

Navigating Life's Path: The Ducts of Destiny:

Life's journey is akin to navigating a network of ducts in an Air-conditioning system, with twists and turns, ups and downs, leading us towards our destiny. Just as ducts guide the flow of air to different spaces, our choices and actions shape the course of our lives, directing us towards our highest potential. Through self-awareness and discernment, we can navigate the labyrinth of existence with clarity and purpose, embracing each twist and turn as an opportunity for growth and evolution.

Sankalpa: The Power of Intentional Living:

In the yogic tradition, the concept of "sankalpa" (intention) serves as a guiding light on our path, much like a map to navigate the ducts of destiny. By clarifying our intentions and aligning them with our deepest values and aspirations, we set a course for success and fulfillment. Like a well-designed Air-conditioning system, where ducts are meticulously planned and laid out, our intentions provide a framework for conscious living, guiding us towards our true north amidst life's complexities.

Building Resilience: Spiritual Insulation for Life's Challenges:

Just as insulation in Air-conditioning ducts prevents energy loss and ensures efficient airflow, our spiritual practices provide insulation against the fluctuations of external circumstances. Through meditation, yoga, and mindfulness, we strengthen our inner resilience and fortitude, shielding ourselves from the turbulent winds of change. As we navigate the ducts of destiny with courage and grace, we emerge stronger and more empowered, ready to embrace the unfolding of our highest potential.

CHAPTER 10

ADAPTIVE COMFORT - EMBRACING CHANGE

Embracing Change: Adapting Like an Air-Conditioning System:

Change is the only constant in life, much like the fluctuating temperatures controlled by an Air-conditioning system. Just as an air conditioner adjusts to varying environmental conditions, we too must learn to adapt and thrive amidst the ever-changing landscape of existence. Through practices like mindfulness, flexibility, and surrender, we cultivate the resilience and adaptability needed to navigate life's twists and turns with grace and ease.

Vairagya: Letting Go of Attachments:

In the yogic tradition, the concept of "vairagya" (non-attachment) encourages us to relinquish our grip on outcomes and embrace the flow of life with equanimity. By releasing our resistance to change and surrendering to the inherent impermanence of existence, we free ourselves from the grip of fear and anxiety, much like a Spiritual Conditioning relinquishing control to the natural rhythms of the environment. As we cultivate a state of adaptive comfort, we open ourselves to the infinite possibilities that arise when we embrace the unknown with an open heart and mind.

Inner Wisdom: Navigating Change with Clarity:

Just as smart technology enables Air-conditioning systems to adapt to changing conditions with precision and efficiency, our inner wisdom guides us to respond to life's challenges with discernment and clarity. Through practices like meditation, introspection, and self-inquiry, we tap into the reservoir of wisdom that resides within us, empowering us to navigate even the most turbulent waters with grace and resilience. As we embrace change as an opportunity for growth and transformation, we step into the flow of life with confidence and courage, knowing that we are capable of weathering any storm that comes our way.

CHAPTER 11

HUMIDITY CONTROL - MANAGING EMOTIONAL MOISTURE

Managing Emotional Humidity: Cultivating Inner Peace:

Just as humidity control is essential for maintaining comfort in Air-conditioning systems, managing our emotional moisture is crucial for inner peace and well-being. Emotions, like humidity levels, fluctuate based on external and internal factors, impacting our mental and physical state. Through mindfulness practices and emotional regulation techniques, we can cultivate the awareness and skills needed to manage our emotional climate with grace and balance.

Vairagya: Observing Emotions with Detachment:

In the yogic tradition, the concept of "vairagya" (detachment) teaches us to observe our emotions without attachment or aversion, much like a Spiritual Conditioning adjusts humidity levels without clinging to any particular outcome. By developing a spacious and non-reactive awareness of our inner landscape, we create space for emotions to arise and dissolve naturally, without becoming overwhelmed or consumed by them. As we cultivate emotional resilience and flexibility, we navigate life's ups and downs with equanimity and ease.

Emotional Dehumidification: Purifying Our Inner Landscape:

Just as dehumidifiers extract excess moisture from the air to maintain optimal conditions, our spiritual practices serve as tools for emotional purification and balance. Through practices like meditation, breathwork, and journaling, we release stagnant emotions and clear energetic blockages, restoring flow and vitality to our emotional landscape. As we attune ourselves to the subtle rhythms of our inner world, we create a climate of emotional harmony and well-being, where peace and joy flourish unabated.

CHAPTER 12

SEASONAL TRANSITIONS - EMBRACING CHANGE

Embracing Life's Seasonal Transitions:

Life is a series of seasonal transitions, each offering its own gifts and challenges, much like the changing seasons in nature. Just as Air-conditioning systems adapt to shifting environmental conditions, we too must learn to embrace change with grace and resilience. Through practices like mindfulness, self-reflection, and adaptability, we navigate the cyclical rhythms of life with ease and equanimity, welcoming each transition as an opportunity for growth and renewal.

Santosha: Finding Contentment in the Present:

In the yogic tradition, the concept of "santosha" (contentment) teaches us to find satisfaction and fulfillment in the present moment, regardless of external circumstances. By cultivating a sense of inner peace and acceptance, we transcend the fluctuations of the external world and find solace in the eternal sanctuary of our own hearts. Like a well-insulated Air-conditioning system that maintains comfort regardless of external conditions, our inner contentment serves as a source of stability and resilience amidst life's ever-changing tides.

Harnessing Inner Wisdom for Adaptability:

Just as smart technology enables Air-conditioning systems to anticipate and respond to seasonal shifts with precision and efficiency, our inner wisdom guides us to adapt and thrive amidst the changing landscapes of existence. Through practices like meditation, visualization, and intention setting, we attune ourselves to the natural rhythms of the universe, aligning our actions with the flow of divine intelligence. As we embrace the ebb and flow of life with openness and trust, we surrender to the wisdom of the seasons, knowing that each transition carries the seeds of new beginnings and infinite possibilities.

CHAPTER 13
ZONING - CREATING SACRED SPACES

Cultivating Inner Sanctuaries for Growth:

Just as Air-conditioning systems utilize zoning to create customized comfort in different areas, we too can cultivate sacred spaces within ourselves for introspection and growth. These inner sanctuaries serve as havens of tranquility and inspiration, where we can retreat from the noise and distractions of the external world to connect with our innermost essence. Through practices like meditation, ritual, and creative expression, we create zones of sacredness within, nurturing our soul's evolution and deepening our connection to the divine.

Dhyana: Entering the Depths of Meditation:

In the yogic tradition, the concept of "dhyana" (meditation) involves entering into a state of deep absorption and communion with the divine, much like zoning allows us to enter into a space of inner stillness and presence. By cultivating awareness and presence in our sacred spaces, we open ourselves to the wisdom and guidance of the universe, allowing divine inspiration to flow freely through us. As we honor the sanctity of these inner realms, we create fertile ground for spiritual awakening and transformation to take root and blossom.

Protecting Our Inner Spaces:

Just as insulation in Air-conditioning systems ensures optimal temperature control and energy efficiency, our spiritual practices provide insulation against the disturbances of the external world, safeguarding the sanctity of our inner spaces. Through practices like mindfulness, grounding, and energetic protection, we create a shield of light and love around our sacred zones, preserving their purity and integrity. As we tend to these inner sanctuaries with reverence and care, we cultivate a deeper sense of connection to the divine within and without, anchoring ourselves in the timeless wisdom of the heart.

CHAPTER 14
SILENT COMFORT - FINDING PEACE WITHIN

Cultivating Silent Comfort Amidst Chaos:

In the stillness of silence lies the deepest comfort, much like the quiet hum of a well-functioning Air-conditioning system provides a sense of peace and tranquility. Amidst the noise and chaos of modern life, it is essential to cultivate moments of silent comfort to nourish our souls and replenish our spirits. Through practices like meditation, contemplation, and solitude, we create space for inner reflection and renewal, allowing the voice of the divine to whisper its wisdom into our hearts.

Embracing Mauna: The Power of Silence:

In the yogic tradition, the practice of "mauna" (silence) is revered for its ability to quiet the restless chatter of the mind and attune us to the subtle whispers of the soul. By withdrawing from external distractions and turning inward, we enter into the sacred chamber of silence, where the mysteries of existence unfold in exquisite beauty and grace. As we surrender to the silent embrace of the divine, we discover a profound sense of peace and contentment that transcends words and thoughts.

Nurturing Inner Peace Through Self-Care:

Just as regular maintenance ensures the optimal functioning of Air-conditioning systems, consistent self-care practices are essential for nurturing the silent comfort within. Through practices like rest, relaxation, and self-reflection, we replenish our inner reserves and restore balance to body, mind, and spirit. As we honor the sacredness of silence in our lives, we create a sanctuary of peace and serenity that serves as a beacon of light in a world filled with noise and distraction.

CHAPTER 15

MAINTENANCE AND SELF-CARE - NURTURING THE INNER MECHANISM

The Importance of Self-Care Maintenance:

Just as regular maintenance is crucial for the optimal functioning of Air-conditioning systems, nurturing our inner mechanism through self-care practices is essential for our overall well-being. Like the diligent upkeep of Air-conditioning components ensures efficiency and longevity, attending to our physical, mental, and spiritual needs enables us to thrive and flourish in every aspect of our lives. Through practices like exercise, nutrition, rest, and self-reflection, we cultivate a deep sense of self-love and appreciation, honoring the sacred vessel that houses our divine essence.

Svadhyaya: The Art of Self-Study:

In the yogic tradition, the concept of "svadhyaya" (self-study) involves introspection and self-inquiry to gain deeper insight into our true nature and purpose. By turning our attention inward and examining our thoughts, feelings, and behaviors with compassion and curiosity, we uncover the patterns and conditioning that shape our experience of reality. Like the meticulous inspection of Air-conditioning components during maintenance checks, this process of self-reflection allows us to identify areas of imbalance and dysfunction, empowering us to make conscious choices that support our growth and evolution.

Flowing Vitality Through Self-Care Practices:

Just as connecting pipes and cables facilitate the smooth flow of energy in Air-conditioning systems, our self-care practices serve as conduits for the flow of vitality and inspiration within us. Through practices like breathwork, energy healing, and bodywork, we clear energetic blockages and restore harmony to our internal systems, allowing life force energy to circulate freely throughout our being. As we commit to the ongoing maintenance of our physical, mental, and spiritual health, we cultivate a state of wholeness and vitality that radiates outward, blessing all those we encounter with our presence and love.

CHAPTER 16

RENEWABLE ENERGY - TAPPING INTO INNER RESOURCES

Tapping into Inner Resources:

Just as renewable energy sources power sustainable systems, we possess an infinite reservoir of inner resources waiting to be tapped. Like solar panels harness the sun's energy to generate power, we can cultivate practices that nourish and replenish our spirit, sustaining us on our journey of growth and transformation. Through practices like meditation, prayer, and connection with nature, we tap into the boundless wellspring of vitality and inspiration within us, awakening to our true potential as divine beings of light and love.

Channeling Prana for Vitality:

In the yogic tradition, the concept of "prana" (life force energy) is revered as the animating principle that sustains all of creation. By cultivating awareness and intention, we learn to channel prana into every aspect of our lives, infusing our thoughts, words, and actions with vitality and purpose. Like a renewable energy source that powers a sustainable system, prana nourishes and sustains us, guiding us towards greater harmony and balance in body, mind, and spirit.

Grounding Through Spiritual Practices:

Just as mounting stands provide stability and support for Air-conditioning systems, our spiritual practices serve as pillars of strength and resilience, grounding us in our inner truth and purpose. Through practices like yoga, tai chi, and qigong, we cultivate a deep sense of rootedness and presence, anchoring ourselves in the timeless wisdom of the earth. As we align with the rhythms of nature and the cycles of creation, we tap into the renewable energy of the universe, awakening to the infinite possibilities that lie within and around us.

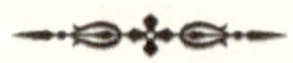

CHAPTER 17

SMART TECHNOLOGY - LEVERAGING WISDOM

Embracing Smart Technology for Spiritual Growth:

In the age of smart technology, we have unprecedented access to information and resources that can support our spiritual evolution and growth. Just as smart Air-conditioning systems utilize advanced technology to optimize performance and efficiency, we can leverage the wisdom of ancient traditions and modern innovations to deepen our understanding of ourselves and the world around us. Through practices like mindfulness apps, virtual retreats, and online communities, we connect with like-minded seekers and mentors, gaining insights and inspiration to support our journey of self-discovery and self-realization.

The Path of Knowledge in Yogic Tradition:

In the yogic tradition, the concept of "jnana" (knowledge) is revered as a path to spiritual awakening and liberation. By seeking wisdom from sources both ancient and contemporary, we expand our understanding of the nature of reality and our place within it. Like a smart Spiritual Conditioning that adjusts to changing environmental conditions, our discernment and intuition guide us towards greater clarity and insight, enabling us to navigate life's complexities with grace and wisdom.

Building Connections for Collective Wisdom:

Just as cables and connecting pipes facilitate communication and coordination within Air-conditioning systems, our connections with spiritual teachers, guides, and peers serve as conduits for the flow of wisdom and support. Through dialogue, collaboration, and shared practice, we deepen our understanding of spiritual principles and integrate them into our daily lives. As we harness the power of smart technology to connect with the wisdom of the ages, we awaken to the truth of our interconnectedness and the limitless potential that lies within us all.

CHAPTER 18

RESILIENCE IN THE FACE OF ADVERSITY - WEATHERING THE STORM

Weathering Life's Storms with Resilience:

Life's journey is marked by moments of adversity and challenge, much like the storms that Air-conditioning systems endure. Just as a well-designed system withstands turbulent weather conditions, we too possess an innate capacity for resilience and strength that enables us to weather life's storms with grace and courage. Through practices like mindfulness, self-compassion, and surrender, we cultivate the inner resources needed to navigate difficult times with resilience and grace, emerging from the tempests of life stronger and more resilient than ever before.

The Inner Fire of Discipline and Determination:

In the yogic tradition, the concept of "tapas" (austerity) refers to the inner fire of discipline and determination that fuels our spiritual growth and evolution. By cultivating a steadfast commitment to our practice, even in the face of adversity, we harness the transformative power of tapas to overcome obstacles and challenges with grace and resilience. Like a Spiritual Conditioning that adjusts to maintain comfort amidst changing conditions, our inner fire of tapas sustains us through life's trials and tribulations, guiding us towards greater strength and self-mastery.

Regulating Energy Flow Through Resilience Practices:

Just as valves regulate the flow of energy within Air-conditioning systems, our resilience practices serve as gateways for the flow of vitality and strength within us. Through practices like breathwork, visualization, and positive affirmations, we activate the body's natural healing mechanisms and tap into the wellspring of resilience that resides within us. As we embrace the storms of life with courage and conviction, we awaken to the truth of our own inner strength and resilience, discovering that adversity is not an obstacle but an opportunity for growth and transformation.

CHAPTER 19
THE CYCLE OF LIFE - EMBRACING IMPERMANENCE

Embracing the Cycles of Life:

Life is a perpetual cycle of birth, growth, decay, and renewal, much like the cycles of operation in Air-conditioning systems. Just as compressors compress refrigerant to initiate the cooling cycle, we too undergo periods of compression and expansion as we navigate the cycles of life. Through practices like mindfulness, acceptance, and surrender, we embrace the impermanence of existence and awaken to the eternal dance of creation and dissolution that unfolds within and around us.

The Wisdom of Impermanence:

In the yogic tradition, the concept of "anicca" (impermanence) reminds us that all things are in a state of constant flux and change. By embracing the transient nature of life, we release our attachment to outcomes and surrender to the flow of existence with open hearts and minds. Like a Spiritual Conditioning that adjusts to maintain equilibrium amidst fluctuating temperatures, our acceptance of impermanence allows us to find peace and contentment in the ever-changing landscape of reality.

Cultivating Stability Amidst Change:

Just as insulation in Air-conditioning systems prevents energy loss and ensures efficient operation, our spiritual practices provide insulation against the fluctuations of life, shielding us from the storms of change and uncertainty. Through practices like meditation, prayer, and self-inquiry, we cultivate a deep sense of inner stability and resilience, anchoring ourselves in the eternal sanctuary of our own hearts. As we embrace the cycles of life with equanimity and grace, we discover the beauty and wisdom that lies within the ever-changing tapestry of existence.

CHAPTER 20

THE ETERNAL THERMOSTAT - DISCOVERING INNER HARMONY

The Essence of Inner Harmony:

At the heart of our being lies an eternal Spiritual Conditioning, guiding us towards inner harmony and balance amidst the fluctuations of life. Like the central control unit in an Air-conditioning system, this inner mechanism regulates the flow of energy within us, ensuring that we remain aligned with the rhythms of the universe. Through practices like meditation, mindfulness, and self-inquiry, we awaken to the wisdom of this eternal Spiritual Conditioning and learn to surrender to its guidance, trusting in its innate intelligence to lead us towards fulfillment and liberation.

Tuning into Our True Nature:

In the yogic tradition, the concept of "satchitananda" (existence-consciousness-bliss) encapsulates the essence of our true nature as eternal beings of light and love. By attuning ourselves to the frequency of satchitananda, we align with the divine flow of existence and discover the inner harmony that pervades all of creation. Like a Spiritual Conditioning that maintains equilibrium amidst changing temperatures, our connection to satchitananda enables us to find peace and contentment in every moment, regardless of external circumstances.

Amplifying Our Inner Guidance:

Just as smart technology enhances the efficiency and functionality of Air-conditioning systems, our spiritual practices deepen our connection to the eternal Spiritual Conditioning within, amplifying its guidance and wisdom. Through practices like energy healing, intuitive development, and spiritual inquiry, we fine-tune our inner instrument and attune ourselves to the subtle whispers of the divine. As we surrender to the eternal Spiritual Conditioning within and allow its guidance to illuminate our path, we discover the profound truth of our interconnectedness with all of creation, and awaken to the infinite potential that lies within us.

With the completion of the 20 chapters exploring the intricate parallels between Air-conditioning systems and human spirituality, the book "Spiritual Conditioning" emerges as a profound exploration of the interconnectedness of the physical and metaphysical realms. Through detailed comparisons, insightful reflections, and practical applications, readers embark on a transformative journey of self-discovery and inner exploration.

Each chapter offers a deep dive into various aspects of both Air-conditioning systems and human spirituality, drawing parallels that illuminate the universal truths underlying both domains. From the regulation of temperature to the management of energy flow, from the importance of maintenance to the resilience in the face of adversity, the book covers a wide range of topics, offering readers a comprehensive understanding of the intricate interplay between the physical and the spiritual.

Throughout the book, readers are invited to reflect on their own lives and experiences, to contemplate the deeper meaning behind everyday phenomena, and to embrace the wisdom that lies within. Whether they are Air-conditioning professionals seeking new insights into their field or spiritual seekers looking to deepen their understanding of themselves and the world around them, "Spiritual Conditioning" offers a wealth of knowledge and inspiration to guide them on their journey.

Ultimately, "Spiritual Conditioning" serves as a reminder of the interconnectedness of all things and the inherent wisdom that permeates every aspect of existence. By exploring the parallels between Air-conditioning systems and human spirituality, the book invites readers to awaken to the profound truth of their own inner Spiritual Conditioning, guiding them towards a life of balance, harmony, and fulfillment.

CHAPTER 21

THE AIR CONDITIONER WITHIN: BALANCING ENERGY AND SPIRIT

Introduction: The Harmony Between Machines and Nature

Imagine stepping into a room after a long day under the hot sun, your skin sticky and your mind fatigued. As soon as you switch on the air conditioner, cool air flows through the room, lifting the heat away and bringing back comfort. Your body, just like that room, also has mechanisms to maintain its inner environment, balancing temperature, energy, and flow to create a harmonious experience. This chapter explores the air conditioning system as an analogy for how our physical bodies and spiritual energy systems operate.

Both are intricately designed to regulate and balance, ensuring that excess energy is neither wasted nor depleted. The human body is like an organic machine, deeply connected with the rhythm of the universe, while an air conditioning unit works within the artificial environments we build. However, their purpose is similar—to maintain a state of optimal balance and comfort.

1. Temperature Regulation: The Body's Natural Spiritual Conditioning

Metaphor: Hypothalamus as the Brain's Spiritual Conditioning

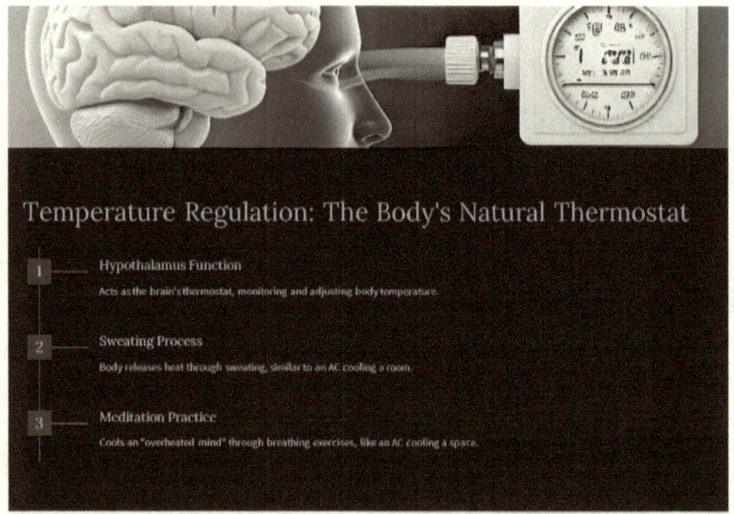

Your body, like a room, needs to be kept at an optimal temperature for peak performance. The brain's hypothalamus functions as the Spiritual Conditioning that constantly monitors and adjusts body temperature, much like the air conditioner's sensor. When your

body becomes too hot, the hypothalamus initiates processes like sweating to cool you down, much like an air conditioner begins cooling the air when the room temperature exceeds a set point.

- Example of Heat Regulation: When you exercise or when it's hot outside, your body sweats to release heat, cooling you down by evaporation. This is similar to how an air conditioner blows out cool air to displace warm air.

Spiritual Connection: Cooling the Overheated Mind

In spiritual practices like meditation, the goal is to cool an "overheated mind." Stress, anxiety, and negative thoughts create internal heat and chaos, much like a room that has been baking in the sun. Through meditation, particularly breathing exercises (Pranayama), you can "cool" your thoughts, returning the mind to a state of balance. This is much like how turning on an air conditioner cools down a space.

Key Quote:

"Be still like a mountain and flow like a great river." – Lao Tzu

Visual Element: A diagram showing the hypothalamus in the brain connected to the body's cooling system. Next to it, an image of an air conditioning unit with cool air flowing through a heated room.

2. Airflow: Circulation of Life and Energy

Metaphor: Air as Life Force (Prana)

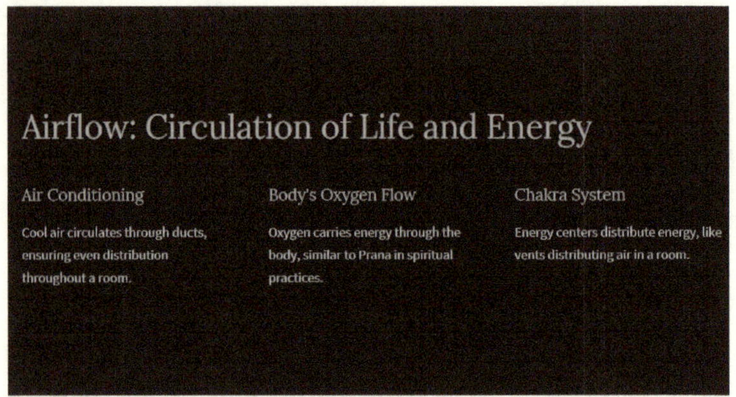

In an air conditioning system, cool air flows through ducts to circulate evenly throughout the room, ensuring no corner is left untouched. Similarly, our body uses air (oxygen) as a carrier of energy. In spiritual practices like yoga and Ayurveda, Prana is the vital life force carried through the air we breathe. Without proper airflow, both in a room and in the body, stagnation occurs. In a house, poor airflow leads to stuffiness, while in the body, lack of oxygen causes fatigue and mental fog.

- Breathing and Energy Flow: Proper breathing techniques, such as deep diaphragmatic breathing, ensure that every cell in the body receives fresh oxygen. This mirrors how an air conditioning unit ensures each room receives fresh air, maintaining an even and breathable environment.

Spiritual Analogy: Chakras and Energy Circulation

In the human body, energy flows through channels known as nadis or meridians, much like air ducts in a house. The chakras, which are energy centers, help distribute energy evenly, much like how vents in a room distribute air. If any of these energy centers become blocked, much like a clogged air duct, energy stagnates, leading to imbalances. Practices like Reiki or chakra balancing are spiritual maintenance techniques that clear these blockages, ensuring the smooth flow of Prana, akin to cleaning out your air ducts.

Key Quote:

"Where attention goes, energy flows." – James Redfield

Visual Element: An illustration of the human body with chakras aligned along the spine, with energy flowing through it, compared to a house with an air conditioning unit distributing cool air via ducts.

3. Filtration: Purification for Optimal Function

Metaphor: Air Filters and Detoxification

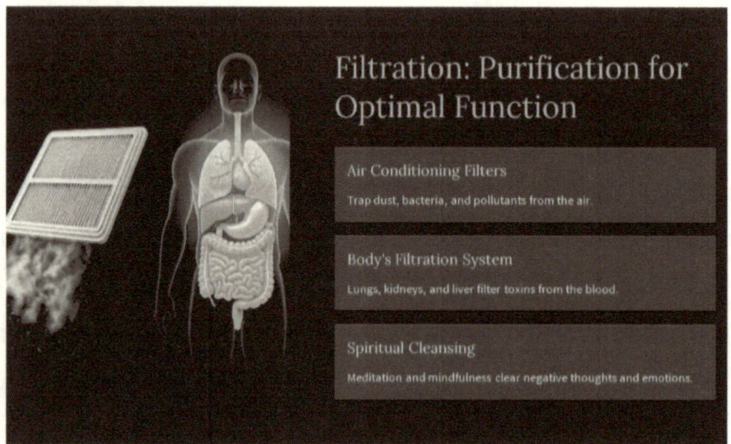

Both air conditioning units and the human body have sophisticated filtration systems. The air conditioner uses filters to trap dust, bacteria, and pollutants from the air. In the human body, the lungs, kidneys, and liver work together to filter out toxins from the blood, ensuring the purity of the body's internal environment.

- Detoxification: Just as air conditioning filters need to be cleaned or replaced regularly, our bodies need regular detoxification through balanced diets, exercise, and hydration. In spiritual terms, practices like fasting and mindfulness meditation help cleanse not just the body but the mind, releasing negative emotions and stress that can cloud our inner environment.

Spiritual Analogy: Cleansing the Spirit

In spiritual terms, just as air filters must be cleaned to maintain optimal airflow, we must cleanse our spirit through practices like meditation, prayer, and mindful reflection. These practices clear the negative thoughts, emotions, and energies that act as blockages, allowing us to experience clarity and peace. A clean spirit is as essential to inner balance as clean air is to a healthy environment.

Key Quote:

"Cleanse your spirit and your body will follow." – Thich Nhat Hanh

Visual Element: A side-by-side comparison of an air filter collecting dust and the human body's organs filtering toxins, paired with an image of someone meditating in a clean, peaceful environment.

4. Energy Efficiency: Conservation and Balance

Metaphor: Metabolism and Energy Use

An air conditioning system operates most efficiently when it is well-tuned, using just the right amount of energy to cool the room without overworking. Similarly, the body's metabolism is designed to use energy efficiently. It converts food into fuel, ensuring that no excess energy is wasted while maintaining enough reserves for daily functioning.

- Balance in Spirituality: In spiritual traditions, energy conservation is equally important. Practices like Yoga, Tai Chi, and Ayurveda emphasize balance and moderation. Overexertion, whether physically or mentally, can lead to burnout, just as running an air conditioner at full blast all day can cause it to wear out prematurely. In life, energy efficiency is about balancing work and rest, effort and relaxation.

Spiritual Analogy: The Importance of Balance

The concept of energy efficiency is deeply embedded in spiritual practices. In Ayurveda, the principle of dosha balance—Vata, Pitta, and Kapha—is central to maintaining optimal health. Just as running an air conditioner at full power when it's unnecessary wastes energy, when we push ourselves beyond our natural limits, we drain our spiritual and physical energy.

Key Quote:

"Moderation is the key to lasting wellness." – B.K.S. Iyengar

Visual Element: A scale balancing two sides—on one side, physical exertion and mental stress; on the other, rest, meditation, and reflection. Beside it, an air conditioner running at optimal efficiency, symbolizing balance.

5. Maintenance and Self-Care: The Power of Tuning Up

Metaphor: Servicing the System

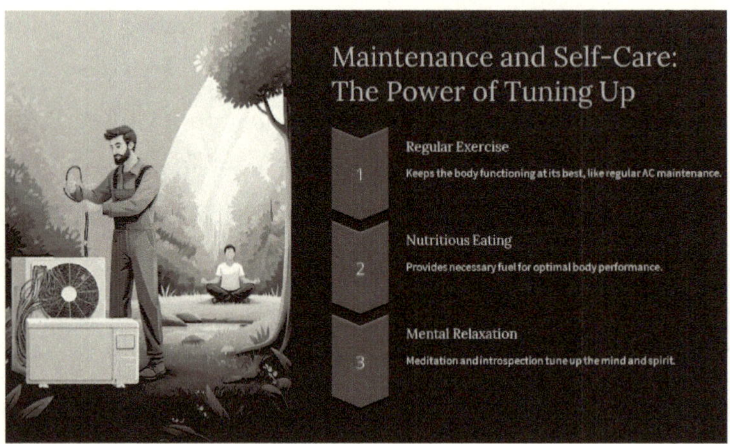

Just like any machine, an air conditioner requires regular maintenance to continue functioning at its best. Without regular cleaning, filter replacement, and occasional tune-ups, it will start to lose efficiency and eventually break down. The same is true for the human body and mind. Self-care practices like regular exercise, nutritious eating, adequate sleep, and mental relaxation are the human equivalent of these maintenance checks.

- Spiritual Maintenance: Practices like meditation, Chakra balancing, and deep introspection are like tuning up the internal air conditioning system. They help keep the mind and spirit running efficiently, preventing energy blocks and emotional burnout. Without self-care, our energy becomes stagnant, just as unmaintained machines become sluggish over time.

Key Quote:

"Take care of your body. It's the only place you have to live." – Jim Rohn

Visual Element: An illustration showing the parallels between a technician servicing an air conditioner and a person engaging in self-care activities like meditation, yoga, and relaxation.

Conclusion: The Cooling Power of Inner Balance

At its core, both the human body and an air conditioning system serve the same function—creating a space of comfort and balance by regulating their environments. The air conditioner cools and purifies the air around us, while the body cools, purifies, and balances the energy within us. By maintaining our internal systems—both physically and spiritually—through proper care, we can live in harmony with our surroundings and ourselves.

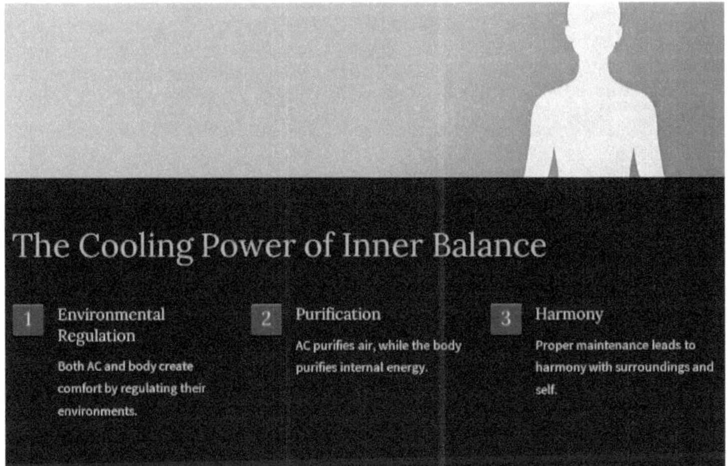

Final Quote:

"The body benefits from movement, and the mind benefits from stillness."

– Sakyong Mipham

Closing Visual Element: A peaceful room where both an air conditioner hums quietly in the background and a person meditates calmly, representing balance between the external and internal worlds.

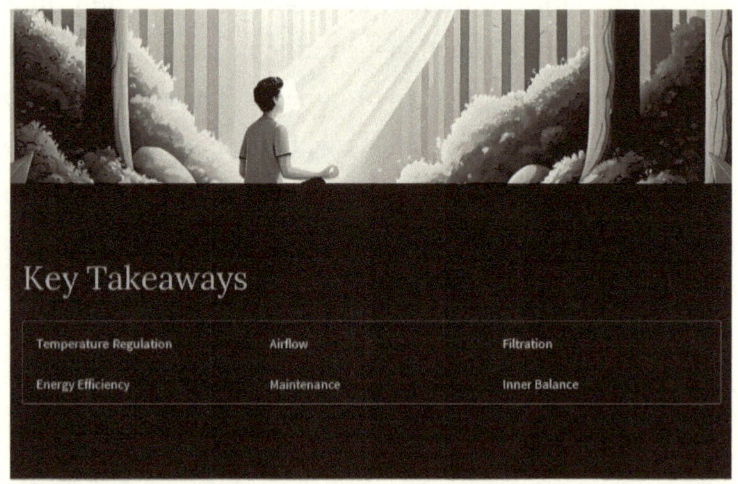

CHAPTER 22

THE SCIENCE OF SWAR GYAN AND AIR CONDITIONING: A DEEPER EXPLORATION INTO SPIRITUALITY AND HUMANITY

In our journey through life, we seek balance—within ourselves and in our surroundings. Two seemingly unrelated systems, Swar Gyan and air conditioning, offer a profound metaphor for this quest. Swar Gyan, an ancient Indian practice of breath regulation, and air conditioning, a technological innovation designed to control temperature, share more than just the concept of balance. When explored through the lenses of spirituality and humanity, these systems reveal profound truths about inner harmony, energy regulation, and our connection to the greater cosmic order.

This deeper understanding helps us bridge the gap between technology and nature, inner and outer worlds, and between individual well-being and collective harmony. By looking closely at how Swar Gyan and air conditioning operate, we can uncover essential lessons about managing the complex dynamics of energy, emotion, and environment. This exploration will not only enhance our personal spiritual journey but also offer insights into fostering a compassionate and balanced world.

1. Swar Gyan: The Ancient Science of Breath

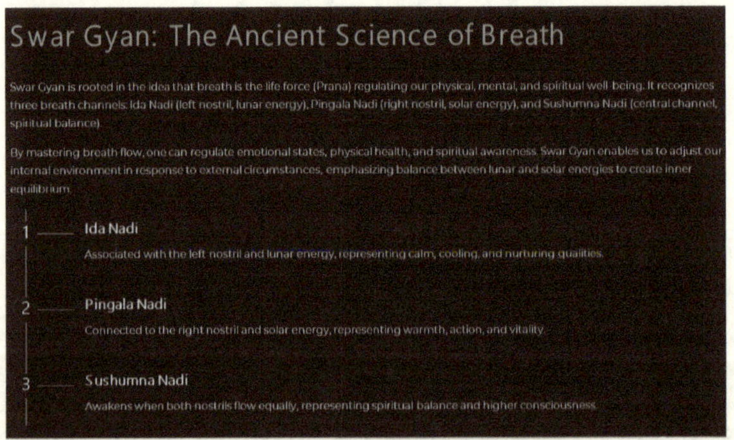

Swar Gyan is rooted in the idea that the breath is the life force (Prana) that sustains and regulates our physical, mental, and spiritual well-being. According to this ancient Indian knowledge, our breath flows through three channels:

- Ida Nadi: Associated with the left nostril and lunar energy, Ida represents calm, cooling, and nurturing qualities.

- Pingala Nadi: Connected to the right nostril and solar energy, Pingala represents warmth, action, and vitality.

- Sushumna Nadi: When both nostrils flow equally, it signifies the awakening of the Sushumna, the central channel, representing spiritual balance and higher consciousness.

The essence of Swar Gyan lies in recognizing which breath channel is dominant at any given time and how it affects our mind, body, and spirit. By mastering the flow of breath, one can regulate emotional states, physical health, and even higher spiritual awareness. Just as a Spiritual Conditioning adjusts room temperature, Swar Gyan enables us to adjust our internal environment in response to external circumstances. This practice emphasizes balance between the lunar and solar energies, creating a state of equilibrium within.

Spiritual Implications of Swar Gyan

On a spiritual level, the breath serves as a vehicle for the individual to transcend the material world and connect with higher states of being. When practiced consciously, Swar Gyan facilitates:

- Inner Peace: As the breath balances the lunar (cooling, calming) and solar (energizing, warming) energies, it creates a peaceful and stable mind, ideal for meditation and self-reflection.

- Higher Consciousness: Breath awareness unlocks deeper levels of consciousness, leading to spiritual awakening. This practice opens up the Sushumna Nadi, leading to states of equanimity, divine connection, and self-realization.

- Unity with Nature: Swar Gyan reveals that we are not separate from the natural world; our breath is in constant interaction with the air that has flowed through other living beings. This interdependence reflects the oneness of all existence, an essential principle in spiritual thought.

2. Air Conditioning: Regulation of the External Environment

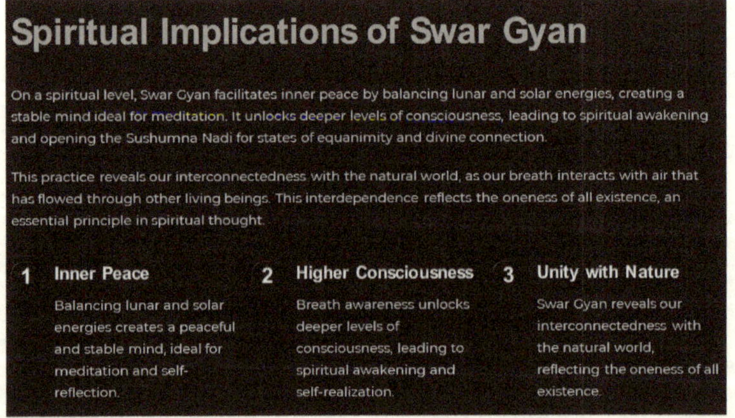

Air conditioning systems regulate the temperature, humidity, and air quality in an enclosed space, ensuring comfort and balance irrespective of the external climate. Air conditioning operates through a combination of thermoregulation, air flow, and humidity control, manipulating these forces to create an ideal environment.

When viewed through a spiritual and metaphorical lens, air conditioning becomes more than a technological convenience. It represents humanity's ongoing desire to create balance and harmony in external spaces while reflecting the internal balancing act required for emotional and spiritual well-being.

Spiritual and Human Symbolism of Air Conditioning

- Regulation of Energy: Just as an air conditioner regulates the energy (temperature) in a space, spiritual practice regulates Prana (life force energy) within the body. Both systems work toward achieving a state of comfort and balance, albeit in different domains.

- Purification: Air conditioners filter the air, removing impurities and toxins. Similarly, spiritual practices such as Swar Gyan and meditation help filter out negative emotions, thoughts, and attachments, purifying the mind and heart for spiritual growth.

- Maintaining Comfort Amid Chaos: Air conditioning enables us to maintain comfort even in extreme weather. In the same way, spirituality teaches us to maintain inner peace and stability, regardless of external conditions—whether they be social, emotional, or environmental challenges.

3. The Commonality: Balance, Regulation, and Harmony

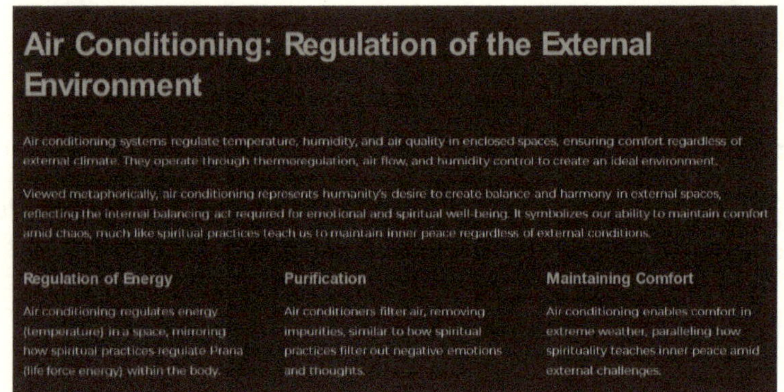

At the core, both Swar Gyan and air conditioning revolve around the theme of balance. While one regulates the internal breath, the other regulates external air, but both strive for harmony—the balance of opposing forces to create an environment where life can thrive.

Regulation and Control

The Spiritual Conditioning in an air conditioner and the breath control in Swar Gyan serve as metaphors for the same process: tuning into the current state of affairs (either external temperature or internal emotions) and making the necessary adjustments to restore balance. When practiced mindfully, Swar Gyan allows us to influence not only our physiological states but also our mental clarity, emotional stability, and even spiritual alignment.

- Ida Nadi (cooling, calm energy) mirrors the air conditioner's cooling function, calming our emotions and regulating overactivity in the mind.

- Pingala Nadi (warming, active energy) mirrors the air conditioner's heating function, energizing and awakening us when needed.

- Sushumna Nadi represents the ultimate state of balance and harmony, much like the ideal room temperature where one feels at peace and comfortable.

Adaptation to External Conditions

Air conditioning adapts to the external climate to maintain internal comfort. Swar Gyan helps us adapt to the external conditions of life—stress, joy, sorrow, excitement—through the conscious regulation of our breath. The ability to stay balanced in the face of changing external circumstances is a shared theme in both systems.

Humanity and Empathy

Swar Gyan teaches us that breath is shared, not just among humans but across all living beings. This shared breath connects us in an invisible web of interconnectedness, fostering empathy and compassion. Similarly, air conditioning represents our human responsibility to create spaces where comfort and dignity are ensured for all. Both systems, when used ethically, can lead to a more compassionate, equitable world where individual well-being contributes to collective harmony.

4. Bridging Spirituality and Humanity

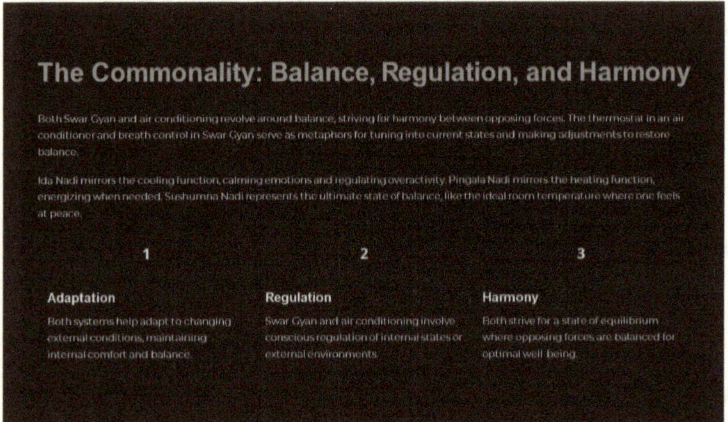

When we explore these systems through the lens of spirituality and humanity, we arrive at a more profound realization: both Swar Gyan and air conditioning symbolize the bridge between inner and outer worlds, between individual well-being and collective responsibility.

Swar Gyan and Spiritual Growth

Through Swar Gyan, we learn that the breath is a microcosm of the universe. The flow of breath mirrors the flow of life energy—as it waxes and wanes, so do our emotional, mental, and spiritual states. Mastering Swar Gyan leads to a deeper understanding of the rhythms of the universe, aligning our breath with the cosmic energies that govern all life.

In the same way, regulating the breath brings about inner balance and harmony, which extends to how we interact with the world. A person who has mastered Swar Gyan is more likely to radiate calm, compassion, and empathy, contributing to a more peaceful and balanced community.

Air Conditioning and Human Responsibility

Air conditioning, while often seen as a technological tool, carries profound implications for human well-being. It represents the ability to regulate and control our environment, but with that power comes responsibility. Just as we regulate our internal environment through Swar Gyan, we must regulate our external impact on the planet and each other. The ethical use of air conditioning, like the ethical practice of breath control, leads to collective well-being.

5. Deepening the Spiritual Connection: Technology and Nature

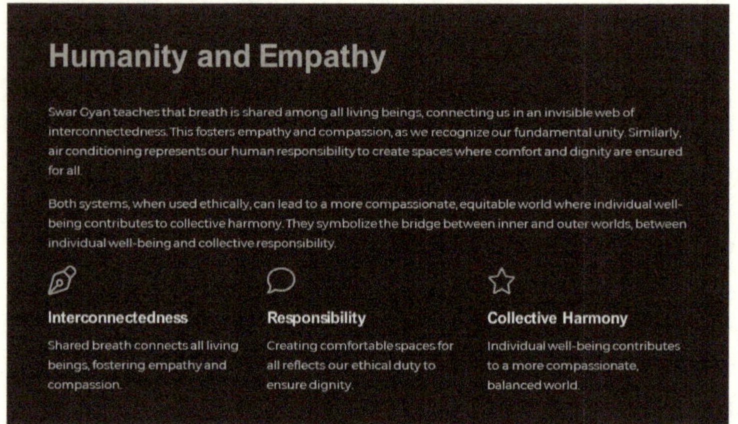

Both Swar Gyan and air conditioning represent a synergy between technology and nature. Swar Gyan, as a natural practice rooted in breath, reflects the rhythms of the cosmos. Air conditioning, as a technological tool, reflects humanity's desire to bring natural forces under control. This balance between technology and nature is crucial for spiritual growth and planetary health.

- Energy Efficiency: In both systems, energy regulation is key. In Swar Gyan, it's about channeling Prana efficiently, without wasting energy on negative thoughts or emotions. In air conditioning, energy efficiency is about reducing waste and creating sustainable environments. Both systems highlight the importance of conserving and directing energy for higher purposes.

- Purification and Growth: Just as air conditioners filter the air, spiritual practice purifies the soul. However, true growth often requires discomfort—working through challenges, emotional healing, and confronting inner truths. Swar Gyan and air conditioning both offer tools for managing this growth, helping us find balance between comfort and transformation.

Conclusion: Harmonizing the Inner and Outer Worlds

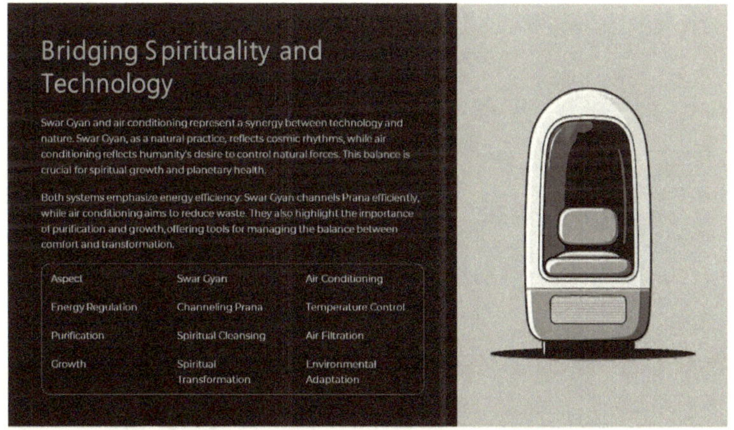

In conclusion, the science of Swar Gyan and air conditioning provides a profound metaphor for the balance, regulation, and harmony we seek in life. Both systems teach us to manage energy—whether it's the breath within or the air around us—in a way that fosters well-being.

But more than that, they reveal the intricate relationship between spirituality, humanity, and nature.

By mastering the regulation of our breath through Swar Gyan, we open ourselves to deeper spiritual awareness, empathy, and peace. Similarly, by managing our external environment ethically through air conditioning, we contribute to the collective comfort and dignity of humanity.

Ultimately, true harmony is found not just in the careful regulation of breath or temperature, but in the deeper understanding that inner balance leads to outer harmony, and individual well-being contributes to collective peace.

Harmonizing Inner and Outer Worlds

The science of Swar Gyan and air conditioning provides a profound metaphor for the balance, regulation, and harmony we seek in life. Both systems teach us to manage energy—whether it's the breath within or the air around us—in a way that fosters well-being.

By mastering breath regulation through Swar Gyan, we open ourselves to deeper spiritual awareness, empathy, and peace. Similarly, by managing our external environment ethically through air conditioning, we contribute to collective comfort and dignity. Ultimately, true harmony is found in the understanding that inner balance leads to outer harmony, and individual well-being contributes to collective peace.

Inner Balance

Mastering Swar Gyan leads to deeper spiritual awareness, empathy, and inner peace.

Outer Harmony

Ethical use of air conditioning contributes to collective comfort and dignity.

Collective Peace

Individual well-being through balanced practices contributes to a harmonious society.

Holistic Approach

Integrating spiritual practices and technological tools for comprehensive well-being.

CHAPTER 23

THE CLIMATE OF WELLNESS: AYURVEDA AND AIR CONDITIONING

Summary

Ayurveda, the ancient Indian science of life, emphasizes maintaining harmony between the three doshas—Vata (air and space), Pitta (fire and water), and Kapha (earth and water). Just like air conditioning adjusts room temperature to comfort, Ayurveda helps balance these internal energies, ensuring optimal well-being.

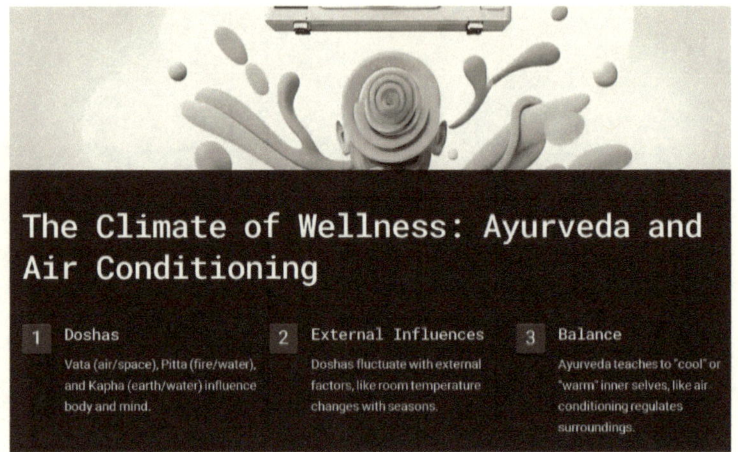

Key Topics:

- Doshas and Their Impact: Each dosha represents different elements that influence the body and mind.

- External Influences: Just like a room's temperature changes with the seasons, our doshas fluctuate depending on external factors.

- The Ayurveda-Air Conditioning Connection: Ayurveda teaches us to "cool" or "warm" our inner selves with specific foods, practices, and routines—like air conditioning regulates our surroundings.

Quote:

"When the body is in balance, it is as refreshing as stepping into a perfectly air-conditioned room on a hot summer day." – Ancient Ayurvedic Proverb

Picture Idea:

An illustration of the human body with overlays of the elements (air, fire, water, earth), with an air-conditioning unit gently balancing these forces around it.

Hashtags:

#AyurvedaHealing #BalanceYourDoshas #ClimateOfWellness #InnerHarmony

Chapter 2: "Yin, Yang, and the Art of Temperature Control"

Summary:

In Taoism, balance is key, just like the Yin and Yang energies that govern the universe. Yin is the cool, passive energy (), while Yang is the hot, active force (). Maintaining a comfortable environment requires regulating these forces—much like an air conditioner balances heat and cold for perfect harmony.

Key Topics:

- Understanding Yin and Yang: These dual forces influence everything in life, from seasons to personal energy.

- Harmony in Life and Nature: Balance between opposites brings peace.

- Air Conditioning and Yin-Yang Balance: Just like an air conditioner fine-tunes the temperature to comfort, so must we adjust our internal energies to achieve inner peace.

Quote:

"The highest good is like water. Water gives life to ten thousand things and does not strive." – Laozi, Tao Te Ching

Picture Idea:

A Yin-Yang symbol in a room where one side is bright and sunny, while the other is cool and shady, with an air conditioning unit seamlessly integrating both environments.

Hashtags:

#YinYangBalance #TaoistWisdom #HarmonizeWithNature #InnerClimateControl

Chapter 3: "The Middle Path to Comfort: Buddhism's Balance in Life"

Summary:

Buddhism teaches the Middle Path, avoiding extremes of indulgence or deprivation. Like an air conditioner, which keeps the temperature just right, the Middle Path ensures a balanced, peaceful life. It's about moderation, staying centered, and finding your inner equilibrium.

Key Topics:

- The Middle Path: How balance leads to inner peace.

- Avoiding Extremes: Both indulgence and deprivation lead to suffering, much like extreme heat or cold makes a room uncomfortable.

- Air Conditioning and Moderation: Like finding the perfect temperature in a room, the Middle Path helps us maintain emotional and spiritual balance.

Quote:

"Just as a candle cannot burn without fire, men cannot live without a spiritual life." – Buddha

Picture Idea:

A serene meditation room with an air conditioning unit subtly balancing the environment. The room symbolizes calmness and simplicity, perfectly tuned to the Middle Path.

Hashtags:

#MiddlePath   #BuddhistWisdom   #ModerationMatters #InnerBalance

Chapter 4: "Cooling the Inner Flame: Sufism's Path to Inner Stillness"

Summary:

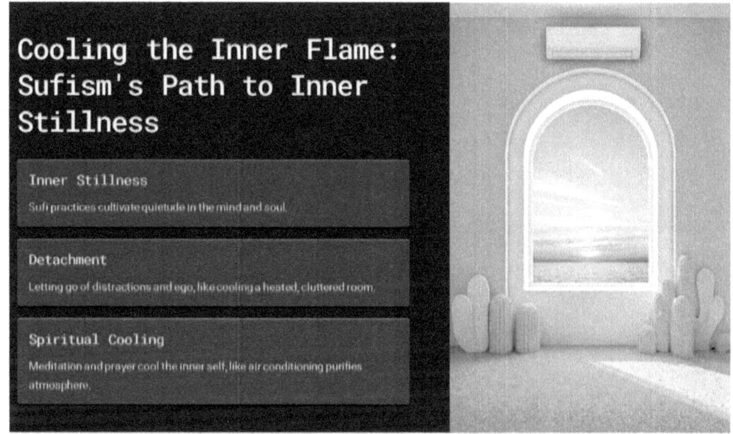

Sufism emphasizes inner stillness and spiritual purity. Like air conditioning that cools a heated room, Sufi practices help calm the soul, quiet the mind, and detach from worldly distractions. Inner peace is akin to that perfect, serene environment where everything feels in harmony.

Key Topics:

- Inner Stillness: Sufi practices cultivate quietude in the mind and soul.

- Detachment and Purity: The spiritual path of letting go of distractions and ego, much like cooling down a heated, cluttered room.

- Air Conditioning and Peace: Just as air conditioning cools and purifies the atmosphere, Sufi meditation and prayer cool the inner self.

Quote:

"Silence is the language of God, all else is poor translation." – Rumi

Picture Idea:

An image of a serene, dimly lit space with a breeze symbolizing spiritual clarity and an air conditioning unit symbolizing the external serenity that mirrors inner peace.

Hashtags:

#SufiWisdom #InnerPeace #StillnessWithin #SpiritualCooling

Chapter 5: "Chakras and Temperature: Aligning Your Energy Like a Perfect Breeze"

Summary:

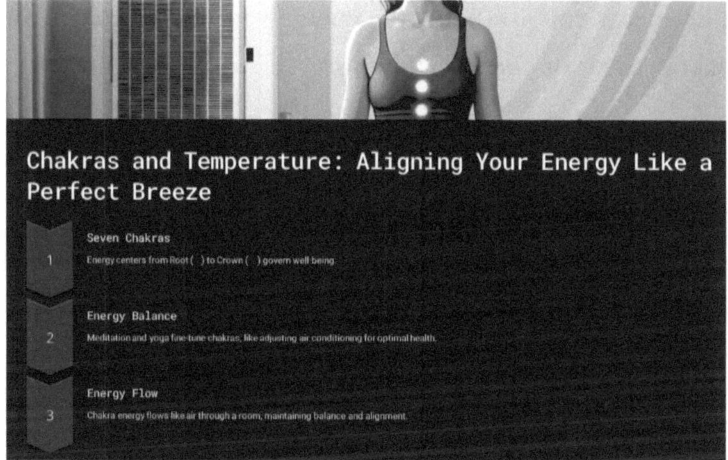

The chakra system refers to seven energy centers in the body that influence our physical, emotional, and spiritual health. Just like air conditioning keeps a room comfortable by adjusting the airflow, balanced chakras ensure a smooth flow of energy, keeping the body in a state of harmony.

Key Topics:

- The Seven Chakras: Understanding each chakra, from the Root () to the Crown (), and how they govern our well-being.

- Balancing Energy: How practices like meditation and yoga are akin to fine-tuning an air conditioning system for optimal health.

- Air Conditioning and Chakra Flow: Just as air flows through a room to regulate temperature, energy flows through our body's chakras, keeping us balanced and aligned.

Quote:

"The energy you give off is the energy you receive. Align your chakras, align your life." – Unknown

Picture Idea:

A person meditating with glowing chakra points along their body, while an air conditioning unit in the background symbolically maintains a peaceful, energy-balanced environment.

Hashtags:

#ChakraHealing   #EnergyAlignment   #BalancedLiving #InnerAirflow

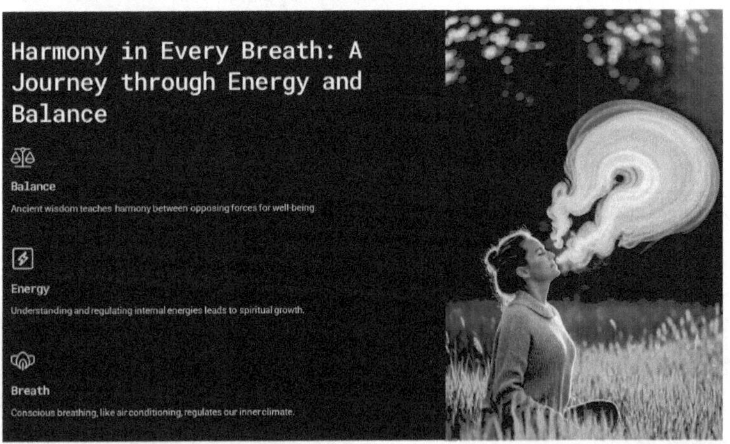

DEEP CONNECTION OF SPRITUAL & AIR CONDITIONING

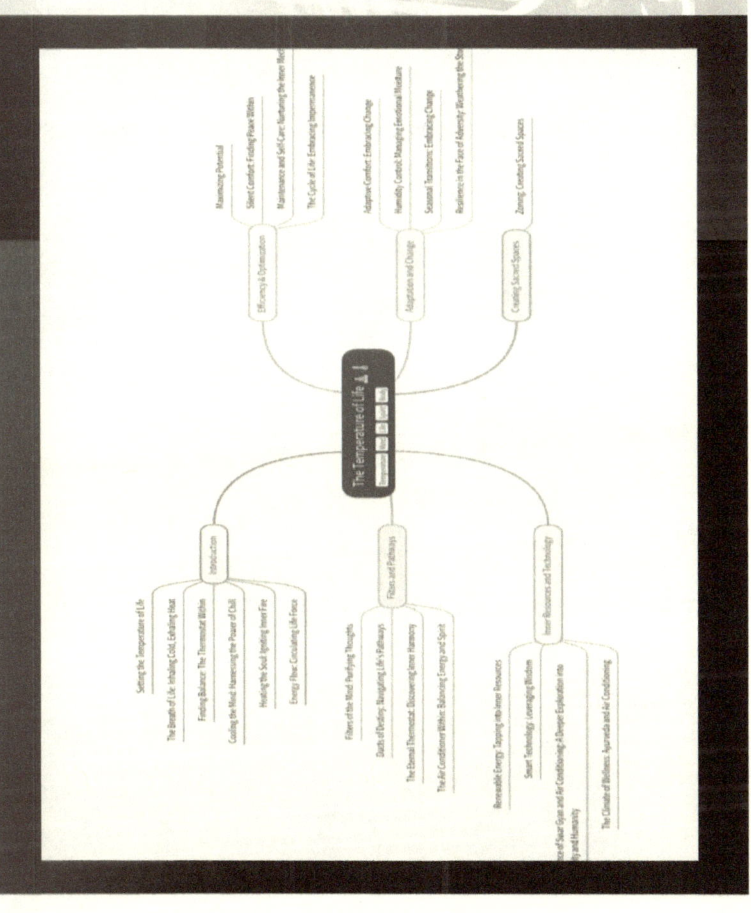

REFLECT & SHARE YOUR INSIGHTS!

"What is the one idea from the book that will stay with you forever?"

Fill in the blank:

The idea of ___________________ will stay with me forever because it taught me ___________________.

Why it matters:

Every book has a lasting impact on its readers. I'm curious to know which idea from my book has left a deep imprint on your heart and mind.

TESTIMONIALS

Anup Tandon, Advisor – Business Development

"Title - Exploring Spirituality through the lens of air conditioning systems. Followed by following : Spiritual Conditioning delves into a novel comparison: the relationship between the mechanical world of air conditioning systems and the abstract domain of spirituality. The author draws unique parallels, inviting readers to consider how intricate machinery, designed to cool and control our environment, mirrors the inner working of the human spirit. Readers who are mechanically inclined or fascinated by the spiritual dimension will find the book intriguing. a very thought - provoking read."

Sooraj Achar, Global Bestselling Author of 25 Books

"Spiritual Conditioning offers a truly unique and insightful perspective on the journey of spiritual growth. Jitendra Khanna brilliantly draws surprising parallels between the mechanics of air-conditioning and the principles of spirituality, making complex

concepts accessible and relatable. Each chapter provides a fresh metaphor for life, balance, and inner harmony, encouraging readers to reflect deeply on their personal spiritual practices. This book is a breath of fresh air, offering wisdom that can cool the mind, warm the soul, and create lasting inner peace. A must-read for anyone seeking both spiritual and personal growth."

DISCLAIMER

materials. Any perceived slight of any individual or organization is purely unintentional.

SPIRITUAL CONDITIONING

Exploring the Interplay of Air-conditioning and Human Spirituality

Jitendra Khanna